A SPY'S GUIDE TO SANTA FE AND ALBUQUERQUE

A Spy's Guide to Santa Fe and Albuquerque

E. B. Held

University of New Mexico Press
Albuquerque

Library of Congress Cataloging-in-Publication Data

Held, E. B.
  A spy's guide to Santa Fe and Albuquerque / E.B. Held.
    p. cm.
  Includes bibliographical references and index.
  ISBN 978-0-8263-4935-4 (paper : alk. paper)
  1. Espionage—New Mexico—Santa Fe—History—20th century.
  2. Espionage—New Mexico—Albuquerque—History—20th
  century. 3. Santa Fe (N.M.)—Guidebooks. 4. Albuquerque (N.M.)—
  Guidebooks. 5. Espionage, Soviet—New Mexico—History.
  6. Espionage, Chinese—New Mexico—History. 7. New Mexico—
  History—20th century. 8. Cold War. 9. United States—Foreign
  relations—Communist countries. 10. Communist countries—
  Foreign relations—United States. I. Title.

  E743.5.H415 2011
  327.1209789—dc22

                            2010035057

Cover: A "shadowy clandestine-operations officer" paying his respects in
front of St. Francis Cathedral, Santa Fe, 2010 (photo by Richard Guy Held).

To Lani Flanagan

Contents

Author's Note

The simple objective of this guide is to make the rich story of twentieth-century espionage in New Mexico come alive for residents of and visitors to the Land of Enchantment.

I am a storyteller, not a trained historian. My hope is to capture the imagination of a wide range of readers, from middle-school students my son's age to retirees like myself, from visitors on a short walking tour to Cold War–history buffs. I have kept the narrative short and crisp in order to appeal to these broad interests. For those who would like to delve deeper into the historical context, I have also included, at the end of each chapter, a Suggestions for Further Reading section.

The main themes of this guide are true beyond a shadow of a doubt. I have not included any detail that is not, to the best of my knowledge, true. Given the murky nature of espionage, however, I do need to reserve an uncertainty factor on some details.

As a retired CIA clandestine-operations officer, I submitted the manuscript for this book to the CIA's Publications Review Board for review as required to prevent disclosure of classified information. I appreciate the assistance the board has provided me. All statements of fact, opinion, or analysis are mine and do not reflect the official positions or views of the CIA or any other U.S. government agency. Nothing in the contents should be construed as asserting or implying U.S. government authentication of information or CIA endorsement of my views. This material has been reviewed by the CIA to prevent disclosure of classified information.

As an employee of the Department of Energy at the time of this writing, I also passed the manuscript through DOE's review-and-approval process, again for the sole purpose of preventing disclosure of classified information.

I would like to express my appreciation to my wife, Lani, and children, Sasha, Sergei, and Nikki; to my friends Elshan Akhadov, Alicia Anastasio, Cindy Barrilleaux, Lucille Boone, Chris Brigman, Chui Fan Cheng, Ken Fisher, Steve and Kara Grant, Ruth Griffis, Cal Guymon, Gerald Hendrickson, Linda Hillis, John Hudenko, Annie Huggins, Daniel Kosharek, Gina Rightley, Al Romig, Marion Scott, Dave Stout, Tammy Strickland, Ferenc Szasz, Annie Tomlinson, Liz Turpin-Puli, Jan Walters, Clark Whitehorn, Marci Witkowski, and Charlotte Wynant; as well as to my colleagues on the CIA Publication Review Board, who must remain unnamed.

Finally, I would like to pay my respects to the honored memory of Adolf Tolkachev; everybody in the world is better off because of his courage and sacrifice.

Key

1. Old Bus Stop
2. Secret Back Entrance
3. Trotsky's Häagen-Dazs
4. Spitz Clock
5. Fuchs/Gold, September 1945
6. 109 E. Palace
7. Bishop Lamy
8. Fuchs/Gold, June 1945

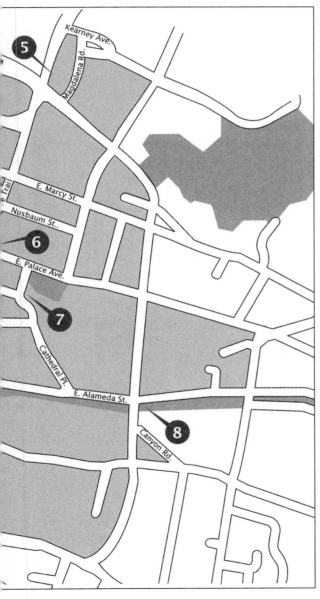

Fig. 1. Espionage sites in central Santa Fe (courtesy of Chris Brigman).

Key

1. Hall/Sax, May 1945
2. Greenglass/Gold, June 1945
3. Hall/Cohen, August 1945

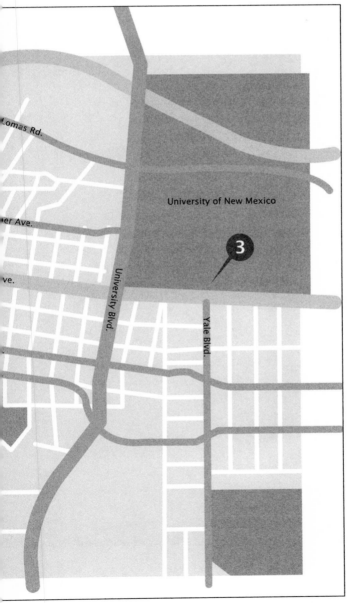

Fig. 2. Espionage
sites in central
Albuquerque
(courtesy of
Chris Brigman).

SANDIA NATIONAL LABORATORIES OFFICE OF COUNTERINTELLIGENCE

The Defection of Edw

Santa Fe, New Mexico

Key

1. Ed and Mary's last supper, September 21, 1985.

2. Mary's reverse.

3. Ed's roll out.

4. Ed and Mary's residence, 108 Verano Loop, El Dorado

→ Defection Route

Lee Howard
September 21, 1985

Fig. 3. Edward Lee Howard's defection route, September 21, 1985 (courtesy of Sandia National Laboratories).

Introduction

Ethics and Espionage

KEY POINT: It may be counterintuitive but is nonetheless true: A powerful nation that holds the moral high ground in the eyes of world public opinion will generally . . . not always, but generally . . . have greater success in the morally ambiguous realm of human espionage than (1) a powerful nation that cedes the moral high ground or (2) a less powerful nation. The reason is quite simple; people around the world will *want* to help a nation that has the power and the desire to influence world events in positive directions, but often those people will want or need to help *secretly*. The history of espionage in New Mexico serves as a case study in support of this ethics-and-espionage conundrum.

Imagine that we are in present-day Santa Fe, New Mexico, having a nice dinner at Geronimo's restaurant on Canyon Road. I point out to you a simply dressed woman in her early thirties dining by herself off to our left. You comment that she looks like a grade-school librarian. I explain that, in fact, she is a prosperous, small-business woman and well-known flamenco singer. She is waiting for her lover, who is a clandestine-intelligence officer operating undercover as a world-renowned scholar. The woman is unwittingly engaged in a conspiracy with her lover and a Nobel Prize–winning poet to assassinate the leading political exile from the repressive regime in—hypothetically—North Korea.

I then point out two college boys in the center of the dining room. You observe astutely that they are both carrying copies of Walt Whitman's poem *Leaves of Grass*, so you assume that they are English literature majors. I explain that, in fact, the younger of the two is a nineteen-year-old Harvard physics prodigy who is in the process of providing secret documents to the older boy on how to construct an atomic bomb. The older boy's secret responsibility is to hand carry the documentation to North Korean intelligence officers at the United Nations in New York City on behalf of North Korean dictator Kim Jong Il. The two boys use Whitman's famous poem as a rudimentary cipher to encrypt their secret communications.

Finally, I point out off to our right a couple in their early thirties gazing out the window. You suggest that they are young parents who have hired a babysitter for the evening so that they can enjoy a dinner date, probably followed by a movie or a walk around the beautiful Santa Fe Plaza. I explain that, in fact, the two are gazing out the window trying to identify the FBI surveillance team that the couple knows is lurking outside, watching their every move. The FBI is on the verge of arresting the young man, a midlevel official of the New Mexico state government, for betraying the two greatest sources of secret intelligence that America has on the North Korean nuclear weapons program. Not wanting to spend the rest of his life in federal prison, the young man has convinced his trusting, young wife to aid and abet his clandestine escape from the FBI surveillance so that he can defect to safety in North Korea. He has promised to send for her and their son once he is comfortably settled in Pyongyang, but in truth he is abandoning her to the FBI.

Of course, you dismissively laugh off my explanations as pure fantasy. None of that "spy stuff" really happens, you say, and it most certainly never happens in New Mexico! Then I explain that if you simply replace each reference to North Korea with the Cold War–era Soviet Union, all of my fantastic stories become matters of historical fact . . . all of which occurred in our remote, little state capital, Santa Fe.

Americans love action-packed spy movies, but as a society, we are uncomfortable with the real, morally ambiguous world of espionage.

Instinctively, most Americans think that spying is wrong, that spies are scum who engage in this wrongdoing for base motives like greed, perversion, or blackmail, and that professional intelligence officers who profit from this wrongdoing, be they CIA or KGB, are at best amoral. These widely held perceptions are only partially true.

Some spies are scum. As we will learn in chapter 9, CIA traitor Edward Lee Howard was a morally unguided alcoholic who did abandon his wife and son when he defected from Santa Fe to Moscow. Greed motivated CIA traitor Aldrich Ames to betray human lives in exchange for money. Psychological perversion motivated FBI traitor Robert Hanssen to betray his country, his family, and his religion.

In stark contrast, Russian scientist Adolf Tolkachev, arguably the greatest spy the CIA ever had inside the Soviet Union, should be a respected hero. As we will also learn in chapter 9, Tolkachev's espionage helped bring the Cold War to a peaceful conclusion. He was motivated as much by love for his Mother Russia as by hatred for the Soviet Union. Tolkachev was arrested after Edward Lee Howard betrayed him and was later executed with one Soviet KGB bullet to the head.

As for intelligence officers, the incidence of amorality among them may or may not be higher than it is among diplomats, politicians, or bankers. Espionage is admittedly a rough-and-tumble business that raises moral dilemmas on a daily basis. Some spies, like Howard, Ames, and Hanssen, can't cope with the ambiguity. By and large, however, professional intelligence officers are public servants guided by their dedication to the national security of their home country, be that America or Russia.

During my career as a clandestine-intelligence officer, I recruited a number of wonderful people to spy on behalf of the United States. Not one of them ever thought that they were doing something wrong. Quite to the contrary, they all thought they were doing something very right indeed.

I paid American tax dollars to all of them in exchange for the secrets they provided the U.S. government. Generally, I did not pay them very much, especially when compared to the value of the information they provided. In a few cases, these spies did earn *substantial* payments of U.S. taxpayer dollars. Money, however, was never their principal motivation.

The spies I recruited were similar to dedicated public servants who did their jobs fundamentally because they felt it contributed to a greater good. *After* they had agreed to commit espionage, I could use money to demonstrate America's appreciation, to help their families, to compensate them for the risks they were taking, and to keep them engaged when the initial thrill of the recruitment wore off. But money was not the reason any of these particular human beings agreed in the first place to commit espionage on behalf of the United States. They agreed to spy because they wanted to help.

I was fortunate that my career as a clandestine-intelligence officer started sometime after the Vietnam War and ended sometime before the present Iraq War. In my opinion, both wars were justified. Nonetheless, it is an unfortunate historical fact that both wars somehow damaged the moral standing of the United States in world public opinion. Between those two wars—the period in which I was active as a clandestine-intelligence officer—America consistently occupied the moral high ground in the eyes of world public opinion, especially when compared to her superpower rival, the Soviet Union.

As a practical matter, America's high moral standing during that time also made it much easier for me to succeed in recruiting people to serve as spies for America and, equally important, made it less likely that I would fail. To understand why, you need some basic training in how intelligence officers recruit spies.

The relationship between a clandestine-intelligence officer and a new spy is as intense as the relationship between lovers. Each relationship is unique. At the same time, courtship of a spy, like courtship of a lover, is characterized by a certain process. The intelligence officer must (1) spot a good target, (2) find some angle to use to recruit this target, and then (3) consummate the relationship by clandestinely collecting secret information from the new spy.

Stage three, the consummation, is quite rewarding and not so difficult. If the CIA could regularly beat the pervasive KGB surveillance to meet with Adolf Tolkachev in the middle of Cold War–Moscow, then imagine how easy it was for the KGB to meet with one of its recruited spies in the relaxed and open environment of American society.

Stage two, the recruitment, is exciting and full of anticipation both for the intelligence officer and for the object of his/her seduction, the prospective spy.

Stage one, the spotting stage, is the wearisome part, during which the intelligence officer is most exposed and, thus, at greatest risk. Not many people make good spies; perhaps one out of one thousand. To be a successful recruiter, an intelligence officer must be aggressive in meeting large numbers of people and quickly assessing them for potential as spies. Unavoidably, the aggressiveness necessary for success also makes intelligence officers stand out to attentive observers. If these observers report their observations to their local counterintelligence authorities, then the intelligence officer will suffer a lower chance of success and a much greater chance of failure.

An intelligence officer in service to a powerful country that occupies the moral high ground enjoys distinct advantages at the first and second stages of this espionage courtship and some advantage even at the third stage. At stage one, attentive observers will be less inclined to report a suspect intelligence officer to the local counterintelligence authorities if that intelligence officer is seen as benign or even admirable. At stage two, recruitment targets will be much more likely to agree to spy for the intelligence officer if they believe that they will be serving some greater good by doing so.

At stage three, the security of an espionage operation depends first and foremost on the clandestine skill and professionalism of the intelligence officer. However, professional intelligence officers from a country that occupies the moral high ground can still be confident that they are relatively at less risk of betrayal from within. Aldrich Ames did betray the CIA from within but, by comparison, imagine the shock in the Kremlin when Ames told them that the CIA had successfully recruited a dozen spies within the KGB.

The story of espionage in New Mexico that you are about to read is permeated by examples of how the moral high ground influences the morally ambiguous world of espionage. Indeed, New Mexican espionage serves as case study for the general ethics-and-espionage conundrum.

It is easy for Americans today to forget that in the 1930s and 1940s the Soviet Union was a powerful nation that occupied the moral high ground in world opinion. During the Depression of the 1930s, and perhaps even more so during World War II, many people considered the Soviet Union the civilized world's best hope against the barbaric regime of Nazi Germany. As a result of that position, in April 1941 the KGB had an incredible 221 American spies, including 49 scientists and engineers.[1]

The atomic scientists who spied in New Mexico for the Soviet Union during the 1940s by no means thought that they were doing something wrong. Very few of those atomic spies accepted any money from the KGB in exchange for the secrets they passed along, which they knew to be of incalculable value. They spied for the KGB because they sincerely, albeit naively, thought it was the right thing to do.

The 1950s and 1960s were not as easy for Soviet intelligence officers operating clandestinely in the United States. Heightened awareness of the Soviet nuclear threat made it significantly harder for the KGB to dupe well-meaning scientists and others into clandestine cooperation. As the horrors of Stalin's Soviet Union became more widely known, Soviet KGB officers looked anything but benign and admirable. American society became less sympathetic to the Soviets and more willing to cooperate with the FBI, America's counterintelligence authority.

American counterintelligence took advantage of this change in the situation by wrapping up virtually all of the extensive spy rings that the KGB *really* was running in the United States. However, in some ways, we also shot ourselves in the foot during this period. The Red Scares propagated by Senator Joseph McCarthy and others did have a basis in fact, but they became so intemperate and xenophobic that they alienated many Americans. Thus, they worked to Soviet advantage by creating a less hostile operating environment for our foreign intelligence adversaries. As we shall see in chapter 8, the case of Los Alamos National Laboratory Director J. Robert Oppenheimer was one of the most egregious of these self-inflicted wounds, one that the KGB persistently tried to take advantage of, even decades after Oppenheimer's death, because the case so infuriated many sincere and loyal Americans. Another self-inflicted wound was Chinese American scientist Tsien Hsue-shen who, chased from America, returned to his birth country to become the father of the Chinese strategic-missile program that now targets America.

By the late 1970s and early 1980s, the world was transformed. It had become increasingly evident to people around the world, including the Chinese, that the Soviet Union was indeed the "evil empire" that President Reagan unabashedly declared it to be. Even clear-thinking KGB officers understood that Reagan was right. Not by happenstance then, the period from 1975 through the demise of the Soviet Union in 1990 was secretly the golden era of American espionage, during which disillusioned KGB officers and other Soviets flocked to the clandestine assistance of the CIA. Also not by happenstance, the genius who catalyzed that golden era of American espionage was a man driven by deep religious conviction who subsequently became a noted public speaker on the ethics of espionage, Burton Gerber.

During 1975–1990, the CIA won the spy-vs.-spy competition against the KGB not because we were any more skilled or professional than they were but quite simply because more people around the world wanted to help us than wanted to help them. Those people wanted to help America win because America had seized higher moral ground than the Soviet Union.

Suggestions for Further Reading

1. *Empires of Trust: How Rome Built—and America Is Building—a New World*, Thomas Madden. Dutton, 2008. A tonic to the negative interpretations of America's role in the modern world that emanate from both the far left and the far right. A scholar of ancient history, Madden argues that both Rome during its republican era and modern America succeeded in establishing "empires of trust" by demonstrating to other people of the world that they would use their power in a restrained and responsible fashion. This book is very relevant to the world of clandestine intelligence.

2. *Fair Play: The Moral Dilemmas of Spying*, James M. Olson. Potomac Books, 2006. Currently a professor at Texas A&M University, Olson is a legend in the CIA. He served as chief in several of the CIA's most important overseas stations as well as chief of CIA counterintelligence. This book is a fascinating look at fifty examples of very real moral dilemmas that face clandestine operations officers on a regular basis.

3. *The Main Enemy: The Inside Story of the CIA's Final Showdown with the KGB*, Milt Bearden and James Risen. Random House, 2003. Remarkable reading for anybody who wants to understand the closing years of the Cold War, although I remain mystified how some of it was authorized for publication. The opening five pages provide a dramatic introduction to Burton Gerber, America's greatest clandestine-operations officer during the Cold War.

4. *Thread of the Silkworm*, Iris Chang. Perseus Book Group, 1995. The sad story of how America chased Chinese American Tsien Hsue-Shen back to China, where he became the father of the PRC's ballistic missile program.

5. *Vaults, Mirrors, and Masks: Rediscovering U.S. Counterintelligence*, Jennifer Sims and Burton Gerber, eds. Georgetown University Press, 2008. In an era of inevitable globalization, this book is as relevant for American corporate leaders as it is for U.S. government policymakers.

Chronology of Atomic Espionage at Los Alamos

January 27, 1944

Ted Hall, an eighteen-year-old physics prodigy from Harvard, arrives at Los Alamos. He has not yet made contact with the KGB. He works as a junior physicist, first helping establish the critical mass of uranium-235 required for a simple gun-type bomb. After it is determined that weapons-grade plutonium is easier to produce than U-235, Hall helps work on the question of whether plutonium can also be used in a gun-type bomb design.

July 11

J. Robert Oppenheimer formally advises Manhattan Project leaders that plutonium will *not* work in a simple gun-type design. Focus at Los Alamos shifts to research on a plutonium implosion-type bomb design.

August 5

David Greenglass, a low-level machinist, arrives at Los Alamos to participate in work on the implosion design.

August 14

Trusted KGB spy Klaus Fuchs, a PhD physicist whose code name is CHARLES, arrives at Los Alamos. His direct responsibility is to help determine whether plutonium can be used in an implosion-type atomic bomb. He expands his access to other secrets by regular attendance at the colloquia that Oppenheimer sponsors to insure free exchange of ideas among Los Alamos senior scientists. He also volunteers to serve as a project historian.

October 25

Ted Hall contacts the KGB in New York City and volunteers to be an atomic spy. He reports to the KGB that Los Alamos is working on not one, but two atomic-weapon designs. The uranium gun-type bomb, he tells them, is simple in design but producing the weapons-grade U-235 is problematic. Weapons-grade plutonium is easier to produce, but a workable implosion design is problematic. Hall's friend Saville Sax agrees to serve as a courier. The KGB gives Hall the code name MLLAD and Sax the code name STAR.

November 29

David Greenglass meets his wife in Albuquerque and agrees to work with his brother-in-law, Julius Rosenberg (KGB code-named ANTENNA) as an atomic spy for the KGB office in New York. The KGB gives Greenglass the code name BUMBLEBEE.

December

KGB reporting suggests that the spy code-named PERSEUS transfers to Los Alamos from the Oak Ridge site in Tennessee. Neither the true name of PERSEUS nor the contribution he or she made to KGB atomic espionage is known publicly (see chapter 8).

Early January, 1945

BUMBLEBEE (David Greenglass) meets ANTENNA (Julius Rosenberg) in New York City and advises that he is working on the implosion-type bomb. KGB–New York is intensely interested in this news, because it confirms what their new source, MLLAD (Ted Hall), reported the previous October. BUMBLEBEE also reports that work at Los Alamos is far behind schedule.

February 16

CHARLES (Klaus Fuchs) meets his KGB contact, ARNO (Harry Gold), in Boston and provides a more optimistic and detailed progress report on the plutonium implosion-type bomb as well as indications that American production of U-235 is progressing satisfactorily. KGB–New York cables a summary of this information, but the complete details do not reach Moscow via diplomatic pouch until early April.

February 28

The KGB updates Stalin on America's atomic-weapons program, based largely on the cautious reporting from MLLAD in October and BUMBLEBEE in January.

Manhattan Project leaders decide on the final design for the plutonium implosion-type bomb. A key remaining problem is designing a reliable initiator.

May 6

MLLAD (Ted Hall) meets STAR (Saville Sax) in Albuquerque and provides an optimistic progress report on both bomb designs. The report includes information that indicates the Americans will have a quantity of weapons-grade U-235 sufficient for one gun-type bomb by August/September 1945 (see chapter 3).

June 2

CHARLES (Klaus Fuchs) meets ARNO (Harry Gold) at the Castillo Bridge in Santa Fe and provides a detailed, comprehensive progress report, including information on the "Urchin" initiator. He also reports that a test of the plutonium implosion-type bomb is scheduled for July 10 (see chapter 4).

June 3

ARNO meets BUMBLEBEE (David Greenglass) in Albuquerque. The meeting is of little substantive importance in comparison to the information provided by MLLAD and CHARLES (see chapter 5).

July 16

Successful test at the Trinity site of the plutonium implosion-type bomb.

August 5

(August 6, Hiroshima time.) MLLAD (Ted Hall) meets his new KGB contact, LESLIE (Lona Cohen), on the University of New Mexico campus in Albuquerque at about the same time as the Hiroshima attack (see chapter 6).

September 19

CHARLES (Klaus Fuchs) meets ARNO (Harry Gold) at the Scottish Rite Temple in Santa Fe and provides a technical report from the Hiroshima and Nagasaki bombings (see chapter 7).

1 Center Stage
New Mexico's Place in Modern Espionage

KEY POINT: The single greatest intelligence coup of the Soviet KGB, their single greatest *counterintelligence* coup, and the planning of their most infamous assassination all took place within one mile of the statue of Bishop Lamy in front of the St. Francis Cathedral in central Santa Fe, New Mexico. Not by coincidence, that statue has been a favorite spot over the years for clandestine-intelligence officers to gather and snap a photo.

When you say "New Mexico," most Americans think of Georgia O'Keeffe landscapes, good food spiced with Hatch green chile, quaint adobe homes with cool inner courtyards, or the "beep-beep" cartoons of Wiley Coyote and Roadrunner. Few Americans think of spy-vs.-spy intrigue.

But say "New Mexico" to certain Russians and see what happens. The very first idea that will pop into *their* minds will be espionage. Indeed, for veterans of the Soviet KGB intelligence service, New Mexico's capital, Santa Fe, qualifies as a sacred city.

Santa Fe first entered the history of modern intelligence in the pre–Cold War period. Zook's, a well-known Santa Fe drugstore, was used as the staging ground for the KGB's most infamous assassination, the 1940 murder in Mexico City of Leon Trotsky, Josef Stalin's archrival for leadership of the Soviet Communist Party. We know this from the astonishing 1994 memoir by Stalin's favorite assassin, KGB General Pavel Anatolievich Sudoplatov.[1] This is the subject of chapter 2.

The Cold War itself began in New Mexico five years later with three seminal events. The first occurred in downtown Albuquerque on Sunday, May 6, 1945. On that day, Ted Hall, a nineteen-year-old American physicist working inside the Los Alamos atomic-weapons laboratory, passed to the KGB key technical details about the Little Boy weapon that would be used at Hiroshima, as well as a progress report on the more effective, but technically more complicated, Fat Man weapon that would be used at Nagasaki. This is the subject of chapter 3.

Four weeks later, on Saturday, June 2, 1945, Santa Fe was the venue for the single most important intelligence success in KGB history. Klaus Fuchs, another Soviet spy working inside Los Alamos, took a Saturday off from work, drove down from the Los Alamos mesa to nearby Santa Fe, and had a brief encounter with Soviet spymaster Harry Gold. During that thirty-minute brief encounter, Fuchs passed to Gold everything that the KGB needed for the Soviets to build their own Fat Man atomic bomb. This is the subject of chapter 4.

Gold should have pocketed his winnings after that brief encounter with Fuchs and returned directly to his KGB base in New York City. Had he done so, the history of the Cold War would have turned out differently. However, Stalin was anxious for even more information about the secret Manhattan Project. The KGB ordered Gold to proceed on to Albuquerque for another clandestine meeting the next day, Sunday, June 3, 1945. That day, Gold met with David Greenglass, another KGB spy working inside Los Alamos. David's sister was named Ethel, and Ethel's husband was named Julius—Julius and Ethel Rosenberg. This is the subject of chapter 5.

In late 1949, American cryptographic analysts working on the top-secret VENONA project deciphered a secret KGB cable. By mistake, the KGB author of the cable used Klaus Fuchs's true name instead of his secret code name, CHARLES. As a result, Fuchs was arrested. He confessed and was essentially given the choice between cooperation with Western counterintelligence or execution. Fuchs chose cooperation. To save himself from execution, Fuchs identified his KGB handler, Harry Gold. Given the same choice, Gold, too, chose cooperation. To save himself from execution, he identified David Greenglass, the man he met only that one time in Albuquerque. Greenglass, in his turn, identified his sister Ethel and her husband, Julius Rosenberg, as his regular KGB contacts.

The Rosenbergs, sincere and devout communist agents, refused to cooperate and were, in due course, executed. The VENONA code breakers also identified Ted Hall as a Soviet spy. Unlike Fuchs, Hall never confessed and was allowed to escape even though the damage he did to U.S. national security was far greater than the direct damage done by the Rosenbergs. All this is the subject of chapter 8.

Forty years later, on September 21, 1985, the final act of the Cold War began, again in Santa Fe. On that Saturday, Santa Fe was the venue for the single most important *counterintelligence* success in KGB history. Edward Lee Howard, a disgraced CIA clandestine-operations officer working at the time for the New Mexico state government, fled Santa Fe and sought asylum in the Soviet Union. In exchange for asylum, he told the KGB about the two most important "mission impossible" operations that the CIA ever ran inside the USSR: GTTAW and GTVANQUISH. When the new leader of the Soviet Union, Mikhail Gorbachev, learned about the incredible details of GTTAW and GTVANQUISH, he knew that the end was near for Soviet communism. President Ronald Reagan knew that Gorbachev knew the end was near. And most importantly, both Reagan and Gorbachev knew that the other knew. This is the subject of chapter 9.

With the demise of the Soviet Union in 1991, many Cold War secrets began to be revealed to the public. In 1994, KGB General Sudoplatov published his astonishing memoir of assassination, disinformation, and atomic espionage. Although he was eighty-seven years old, Sudoplatov could not resist lacing his memoir with an entirely new dose of KGB disinformation. He falsely alleged that other prominent American scientists working at Los Alamos, including J. Robert Oppenheimer, had passed secret messages to the KGB via Zook's, the Santa Fe drugstore that had been used to plan the Trotsky assassination. The following year, 1995, CIA Director John Deutsch effectively responded to Sudoplatov by declassifying the VENONA project. On one hand, the declassified transcripts debunked Sudoplatov's allegations against Oppenheimer. On the other hand, the transcripts proved beyond a shadow of a doubt to the American public that Julius and Ethel Rosenberg had, indeed, been Soviet spies.

Finally, in 1999, eight years after the demise of the Soviet Union, the entire cycle seemed to be starting all over again. In that year, another scientist working at Los Alamos, Dr. Wen Ho Lee, was arrested on suspicion of espionage, but, in his case, on behalf of America's newest great state rival, the People's Republic of China. As with Oppenheimer and the Rosenbergs, much secret information will have to be declassified before we, the American public, can truly understand what happened in the Wen Ho Lee case. It took over forty years for VENONA to be declassified; I personally hope it will not take that long this time. This is the subject of chapter 10.

The espionage events noted above profoundly affected the history of the United States and of New Mexico during the twentieth century. However, because of their clandestine nature, no plaques mark the spots where they occurred. The objective of this guide is to address that situation before all memory of the details is lost.

2 Planning the Assassination of Trotsky | Santa Fe, 1940

WHERE: Santa Fe Plaza, 56 East San Francisco Street; currently a Häagen-Dazs ice cream store; from 1913 until the early 1990s, it was Zook's Drugstore.

WHAT: In 1940, Zook's Drugstore served as a base and safe haven for KGB operatives planning the assassination of Leon Trotsky in Mexico City.

In early 1939, Soviet dictator Josef Stalin was angry and suspicious. Two years earlier, he had ordered the foreign-intelligence directorate of the KGB to assassinate his political rival, Leon Trotsky.[1] Trotsky, not Stalin, had been the heir apparent when the founder of the Soviet Union, Vladimir Lenin, died in 1924. It was Trotsky, not Stalin, who had organized the Red Army and miraculously saved the Bolshevik Revolution during the Civil War of 1917–1920. It was Trotsky, not Stalin, who was the idol of the international communist movement due to his support for revolutionary movements worldwide. Despite Trotsky's strong position, in 1929 Stalin was able to force him to flee the Soviet Union into political exile—but that was not enough. Stalin wanted Trotsky dead.

Stalin knew that Trotsky still had supporters in Moscow and suspected that the KGB's failure to carry out the assassination as ordered was indication of an anti-Stalin/pro-Trotsky plot. Stalin's paranoia was skillfully encouraged by Hitler's malevolent intelligence chief, Reinhard Heydrich, who cast doubts on the loyalty of the Soviet KGB leadership with well-placed bits of Nazi German disinformation. (Heydrich is historically infamous as the chairman of the 1942 Wannsee Conference, the architect of the Holocaust, and as the man who coined the evil phrase "the Final Solution.") Manipulated by Heydrich, Stalin ordered the arrest and execution of hundreds of senior KGB officers, particularly those who had served overseas in the KGB's foreign intelligence directorate.[2]

General Pavel Anatolievich Sudoplatov was one such senior KGB officer. Sudoplatov had made himself a name as a KGB specialist in "special tasks," like assassination, sabotage, and deception. (The assassination he was most proud of involved his personally presenting a bomb disguised as a box of the victim's favorite chocolates.) Now, Sudoplatov watched as many other KGB friends and assassins were themselves accused of being "enemies of the people," summarily tried, and then shot. Sudoplatov was expecting the same fate to befall him at any moment. So, in March 1939, when he received a summons to report immediately to the office of Stalin's newly appointed KGB chief, Lavrenti Beria, General Sudoplatov was convinced that his own death was near.

Sudoplatov entered Beria's office and responded meekly when the KGB chief berated him for laziness. Beria then ordered Sudoplatov to accompany him to an unspecified meeting. They went down to Beria's awaiting limousine, drove a short distance from KGB headquarters, through the Kremlin's Spassky Gate, and stopped at the famous dead end just off Ivanovsky Square. Only then did Sudoplatov realize that he was not on the way to prison but rather that he and Beria had been summoned to a private meeting with the dictator, Josef Stalin himself.

Stalin did not waste much time getting to the point. He explained the strategic reasons why it was important for his personal nemesis, Leon Trotsky, to be assassinated in a fashion that could not be attributed to Moscow. He noted that in 1937 he had given this important assignment to former KGB chief Nikolai Yezhov and Yezhov's trusted aide, KGB General Sergei Shpigelglas. They had failed to carry out their assignment and, accordingly, had been executed themselves. Stalin explained that he was now giving this important assignment to Beria and Beria's trusted aide, KGB General Sudoplatov. Stalin said that Sudoplatov would be provided with whatever assistance and support he needed and directed that the assassination should be carried out within a year. With no further questions, Beria and Sudoplatov were abruptly dismissed.

In his remarkable 1994 memoir, *Special Tasks*, Sudoplatov admits to feeling a strange enthusiasm for eliminating Trotsky, a man he had never met, before Stalin eliminated Sudoplatov!

In 1939–1940, Trotsky was living in Mexico City in a heavily guarded compound. As Stalin suspected, Trotsky did have spies inside the KGB who had warned him about Stalin's assassination order. This was not a problem, however, because the KGB also had spies inside the heavily guarded Mexico City compound who provided detailed intelligence on Trotsky's movements and the security arrangements in place to protect him.

To execute his orders, General Sudoplatov faced two key operational problems: (1) how to gain access to the compound in order to assassinate Trotsky and (2) how to carry out the assassination in a fashion that could not be attributed to Moscow. To these ends, Sudoplatov first decided to organize the assassination independently of official Soviet government facilities in Mexico and the United States. Sudoplatov decided that he would use KGB operatives under "non-official cover." Such operatives are referred to as "illegals" by Russians and as "NOCs" by Americans. (In the famous scene in the first *Mission Impossible* movie, Tom Cruise descends on a wire into the computer room in order to steal the "NOC List.")

The illegal/NOC that Sudoplatov chose to lead the Trotsky operation was perfect. He was not even a Soviet citizen. He was an Argentine of Lithuanian ancestry. Josef Grigulevich, code-named PADRE, is one of the most legendary field operatives in KGB history. His father had emigrated from Lithuania to Argentina and there founded a successful chain of drugstores. Josef was recruited by the KGB when he was at university in Paris. He first made his reputation leading KGB assassination-and-sabotage teams operating against suspected Trotskyites in Spain during the 1936–1939 civil war. In 1940, he organized the assassination of Trotsky himself. Later, under the alias Teodoro Castro, he maneuvered himself into being named the Costa Rican ambassador to the Vatican. In this latter role, Grigulevich was ordered by Stalin to assassinate Joseph Broz Tito, the anti-Stalinist leader of Yugoslavia. Stalin himself died, however, before Grigulevich made any attempt on Tito.[3] After retiring from the KGB, Grigulevich became a renowned scholar of Latin American history, publishing fifty-eight books.

Like all successful assassins, Grigulevich's first concern was to insure his own escape from the assassination scene. Since the scene of the Trotsky assassination would be Mexico City, Grigulevich laid out a plan to escape north from Mexico City and across the border into the United States. Since he was of Lithuanian ancestry and had connections in the drugstore business, Grigulevich searched his contacts for others of Lithuanian ancestry in the drugstore business located somewhere in the southwestern United States. He found Zook's Drugstore in the small town of Santa Fe, New Mexico, owned by John Zook and managed by John's only child, Katie.[4]

John Zook, born in Lancaster County, Pennsylvania in 1875, was of Lithuanian ancestry. He graduated from the Philadelphia College of Pharmacy in 1895, worked in New York City and Pueblo, Colorado, and settled in Santa Fe in the early 1900s. In 1906, he married Zelma Brown. The same year, Zook became part owner of Ireland's (later Capital) Pharmacy. In 1908, he opened his own pharmacy, Zook's, and in 1913, he expanded into larger facilities at 56 East San Francisco Street, just off the main plaza in Santa Fe. John Zook died in 1950 at age seventy-five.

Katherine Zook, John and Zelma's only child, was born in 1907. Katie became a well-known figure in Santa Fe society, famous for her erect carriage, long braids coiled on her head, and her love for fancy hats. She was often seen around town on her daily walks with her beloved dog, Tillie, or driving her bright-red convertible. She traveled the world extensively. She never married.[5]

When Grigulevich came knocking in 1940, John Zook was sixty-five and in semiretirement; Katie, thirty-three, was managing the family drugstore. Grigulevich was twenty-seven, cosmopolitan, and a ladies' man akin to James Bond. There are no available public records to provide insight into any personal relationship between Katie and Grigulevich. She most likely didn't even know his true name.

The physical aspects of Zook's Drugstore fit Grigulevich's needs perfectly. The building was centrally located, which allowed people to come and go with ease. At the same time, it was not directly on the Santa Fe Plaza, complicating the task of police or counterintelligence officers conducting exact surveillance of any-one coming and going.

The physical detail that would have most attracted Grigulevich was the hidden back entrance to the building, which was one floor down from the front entrance on San Francisco Street and totally hidden from view. It opened onto a small courtyard behind what is now the restaurant Pasquale's and from there onto Water Street just east of Don Gaspar Avenue. A casual observer would never guess that somebody walking from this courtyard on to Water Street might have gotten there from Zook's entrance moments before. Conversely, a police or counterintelligence officer watching people going into Zook's main entrance on San Francisco Street would have no way of observing anyone leave by the hidden back entrance just moments later. Buildings with double entries like this just warm the cockles of a spy's heart!

Having prepared his escape, Grigulevich was ready to plan the assassination.

Under an operational umbrella code-named OPERATION DUCK, General Sudoplatov and NOC Grigulevich developed two separate tactical plans to assassinate Trotsky. One plan relied on the famous Mexican painter David Siqueiros, a staunch supporter of Stalin and one of the founders of the Mexican Communist Party. The other relied on Ramon Mercader, a Spanish aristocrat whose ancestors included a Spanish governor of Cuba and a Spanish ambassador to the czar. Like Grigulevich, both Siqueiros and Mercader had become KGB operatives during the Spanish Civil War. Neither of them knew Grigulevich's true name.

The first attempt against Trotsky occurred in the predawn hours of May 23, 1940. Grigulevich had befriended a wealthy, idealistic young American named Sheldon Harte, who was serving as a volunteer secretary and bodyguard for Trotsky. When Harte unwittingly opened the compound gate to allow his "friend" Grigulevich to enter, Siqueiros and two-dozen armed men stormed through. They thoroughly machine gunned the bedroom where Trotsky and his wife were sleeping . . . but somehow managed to miss them completely. Harte was less fortunate. Since he could identify Grigulevich, he was taken away and executed. His body was discovered a few days later dumped in a lime pit beside a road.

Grigulevich disappeared, presumably slipping across the American border and hiding out in Santa Fe with Katie Zook. Siqueiros was briefly arrested and accused of the attempted assassination. He escaped from Mexico to Chile thanks to the assistance of the well-known poet Pablo Neruda, at the time the Chilean consul general to Mexico and another staunch supporter of Stalin.

The second, successful attempt against Trotsky occurred three months later, on August 20. Mercader, operating in alias as a Canadian businessman named Frank Jackson, had insinuated himself into Trotsky's circle by seducing Trotsky's secretary, Sylvia Ageloff. Sylvia arranged an appointment for "Frank" with Trotsky, during which Frank pulled out a pickax and plunged it into Trotsky's brain. Trotsky died the next day.

"Frank Jackson" was arrested and jailed for twenty years. The Mexicans did not discover his true identify until 1946. Even then, Mercader continued to stick to his pre-arranged cover story that he had killed Trotsky because Trotsky had denied permission for Frank to marry Sylvia. Mercader never revealed that he was acting on KGB orders, but after his release from Mexican prison on August 20, 1960, Mercader fled to the Soviet Union, where then-KGB Chief Aleksandr Nikolayevich Shelepin decorated him as a Hero of the Soviet Union.

Grigulevich laid low in Santa Fe until 1941 and then parted company with Katie Zook. In his memoirs, General Sudoplatov makes dubious allegations that the KGB continued to use Zook's Drugstore as part of its atomic-espionage program against Los Alamos. We will discuss these allegations in greater detail in chapter 7.

Suggestions for Further Reading

1. *Special Tasks: The Memoirs of an Unwanted Witness—A Soviet Spymaster,* Pavel Anatolievich Sudoplatov et al. Little Brown and Company, 1994. The unabashed memoirs of Stalin's chief assassin. Self-serving and replete with disinformation about Soviet espionage in the United States, Sudoplatov's memoirs nonetheless provide astonishing insight into the honored tradition that plausibly deniable assassinations still have inside Russian intelligence. Sudoplatov's tone in this book is in stark contrast to that of Jim Olson's book *Fair Play.*

2. *The Sword and the Shield: The Mitrokhin Archive and the Secret History of the KGB,* Christopher Andrew and Vasili Mitrokhin. Perseus Book Group, 1999. A detailed history of the KGB based on caseloads of secret documents

smuggled out of Russia in 1992 by KGB archivist Vasili Nikitich Mitrokhin and as essential as the VENONA transcripts to an understanding of the Cold War. Chapter 5, "Terror," discusses Grigulevich and his central role in the Trotsky assassination.

3. *The Haunted Wood: Soviet Espionage in America during the Stalin Era*, Allen Weinstein and Alexander Vassiliev. Random House, 1999. The definitive reference on Soviet espionage in America from the 1930s through the early 1950s, based on the VENONA transcripts and KGB files from the era. To my mind, the single most trustworthy reference available.

3 The Cold War Begins
Albuquerque, May 6, 1945

WHERE: The intersection of Central Avenue and First Street in downtown Albuquerque.

WHAT: In the vicinity of this intersection on Sunday, May 6, 1945, atomic spy Ted Hall (code-named MLLAD) met his best friend, Saville Sax (code-named STAR). Sax had volunteered to serve as a secret courier between Hall and the New York City office of the KGB. Hall provided Sax information on the critical mass of uranium-235 needed in the Little Boy atomic-bomb design that would eventually be used at Hiroshima, as well as a progress report on the implosion technique used in the plutonium-based Fat Man design that would be used at Nagasaki. Sax delivered this information to KGB officer Anatoli Yatskov in New York City on Friday, May 11.[1]

In the fall of 1944, Soviet dictator Josef Stalin was angry again. Stalin knew that America's Manhattan Project was on the verge of developing an atomic bomb, which the KGB had code-named ENORMOZ. Stalin also knew that the KGB had recruited four spies who were working inside America's top-secret atomic bomb laboratory. The four atomic spies were code-named MLLAD, CHARLES, BUMBLEBEE, and PERSEUS.[2]

Stalin was angry, first because the KGB had failed to obtain sufficient detailed and timely secret information from the four spies to help the Soviet's fledgling program of theoretical research for its own ENORMOZ. The second reason Stalin was angry was that the KGB had failed to recruit a fifth atomic spy, a man code-named CHESTER. Stalin had a low tolerance for failure and so, once again, turned to General Sudoplatov to take charge.

Sudoplatov recognized that the first KGB failure was the result of clever planning by American counterintelligence. In late 1942, when the site for this top-secret atomic-bomb laboratory was being selected, the most logical choices were (1) outside New York City, close to Harold Urey of Columbia University and Albert Einstein of Princeton University, (2) outside Chicago, close to Enrico Fermi of the University of Chicago, or (3) outside San Francisco, close to Ernst Lawrence of the University of California, Berkeley.[3] One of the main reasons those sites were not selected was that there were active KGB offices in New York, Chicago, and San Francisco.

To counter the efforts of the KGB and other foreign-intelligence adversaries, clever American counterintelligence officials decided to locate this top-secret laboratory in the middle of nowhere. That way, even if the KGB succeeded in recruiting spies working inside the laboratory, the KGB would have difficulty communicating with them. In contrast to James Bond–fantasies, real-world espionage is all about communication. If well-placed spies cannot communicate secret information to their spy masters, they can do no harm. American counterintelligence knew this just as well as General Sudoplatov.

Sudoplatov did not even try to explain the second KGB failure—not recruiting the fifth spy—to Stalin, however, because it was simply inexplicable. This man CHESTER had superb access to secret information about the atomic-bomb project. Not only that, but he himself had been a communist sympathizer. His wife was a former member of the Communist Party. His brother was a former member of the Communist Party. His best friend was an active member of the Communist Party and in contact with the KGB. Even his mistress was a communist. Sudoplatov simply could not explain why the KGB was incapable of recruiting a fellow traveler like CHESTER to be a Soviet spy.

The "middle of nowhere" site that was finally selected for America's atomic-bomb laboratory in late 1942 was Los Alamos, New Mexico, a beautiful mesa thirty miles northwest of Santa Fe, isolated among the ponderosa pines of the Jemez Mountains with only one, easily guarded road in and out. The selection was largely determined by the thirty-eight-year-old scientist who had been chosen to direct the laboratory, J. Robert Oppenheimer. For twenty years, Oppenheimer had been spending vacations in northern New Mexico at a cabin his family owned on the Pecos River. He had camped, hiked, and traveled on horseback throughout the forested mountains and high-desert wilderness areas of the region. The state served as a physical as well as psychological refuge for him. Oppenheimer knew the state and its people well, and he loved them. This was important, because in selecting the site for his secret laboratory, Oppenheimer was also selecting the site for his own prison.

The choice of Oppenheimer as the laboratory director had raised eyebrows among American counterintelligence officers. Oppenheimer, himself, had been a communist sympathizer. His wife was a former member of the Communist Party. His brother was a former member of the Communist Party. His best friend, Haakon Chevalier, was an active member of the Communist Party and allegedly tried to recruit Oppenheimer in 1942 on behalf of the KGB. Even his mistress was a communist. Oppenheimer was, in fact, the elusive CHESTER the KGB so badly wanted to recruit as a spy—but never did.[4]

The military head of the Manhattan Project, General Leslie Groves, was well aware of Oppenheimer's history as a communist sympathizer but was convinced that Oppenheimer was key to the success of America's atomic-bomb program. So Groves and Oppenheimer essentially made a deal: Oppenheimer would be named laboratory director but would live isolated in New Mexico. Any time he traveled outside the laboratory, Oppenheimer would be accompanied by a team of bodyguards whose first responsibility was to monitor any and all contacts of the illustrious scientist.

This monitoring included Oppenheimer's final rendezvous in San Francisco with his mistress, Jean Tatlock, on June 14, 1943. Oppenheimer spent the night with Jean while his guards waited in a car parked out front. That night Oppenheimer evidently told Jean that his official responsibilities precluded him from continuing their affair. This drove her into a deep depression and six months later she committed suicide. Some believe that Oppenheimer named the test site for the first atomic explosion "Trinity" in tribute to Jean. He drew the name from a John Donne poem that they both loved.[5]

Batter my heart, three person'd God, for you
As yet but knock, breathe, shine and seek to mend

The four spies working inside Los Alamos were supposed to report their secrets to the KGB office, or *rezidentura*, in New York City. Anatoli Antonovich Yatskov was the KGB officer in New York responsible for the three atomic spies code-named MLLAD, CHARLES, and PERSEUS. Aleksandr Semyonovich Feklisov was the KGB officer in New York responsible for the atomic spy BUMBLEBEE. Yatskov and Feklisov were best friends. (An historical curiosity is that Yatskov's brother, Pavel, was one of the KGB officers who met with Lee Harvey Oswald in Mexico City in September 1963, seven weeks before Oswald assassinated President Kennedy.[6] Feklisov, for his part, eventually became the senior KGB officer, or *rezident*, in Washington, D.C., and in October 1962, served as the key intermediary between President Kennedy and Soviet Premier Khrushchev in resolving the Cuban Missile Crisis.[7])

In 1945, American counterintelligence restricted the travel of Soviet diplomats so neither Yatskov nor Feklisov could travel from New York City to New Mexico. Just as Sudoplatov had done with the Trotsky assassination, Yatskov and Feklisov had to rely on NOC officers to help them. The illegal/NOC officer responsible for the atomic spy CHARLES was himself code-named ARNO. The illegal/NOC officer responsible for the atomic spy code-named BUMBLEBEE was himself code-named ANTENNA. The illegal/NOC officer responsible for atomic spy code-named PERSEUS was herself code-named LESLIE. Due to security concerns, however, the KGB had not yet named an illegal/NOC officer to meet with the atomic spy code-named MLLAD.[8]

MLLAD was a mere teenager who had volunteered to work as a spy for the KGB office in New York City a few months previously, on October 25, 1944.[9] The KGB knew almost nothing about MLLAD; Yatskov had never even met him. Yatskov had only met MLLAD's best friend, a twenty-year-old code-named STAR.

STAR had provided Yatskov a technical report, allegedly written by MLLAD, that appears to have been the very first information that the KGB had received directly from a source inside Los Alamos. In the report, MLLAD claimed that he had been assigned to the secret laboratory since January 1944 and had been directly involved in working on not one, but two approaches for an atomic weapon. The first simple approach was based on uranium-235. The second more promising but more complicated approach was based on plutonium. MLLAD's report intrigued Soviet atomic scientists back in Russia, who previously had only received reports of the simple uranium-based bomb. General Sudoplatov, however, feared the report was a trap by American counterintelligence.

Sudoplatov suspected that American counterintelligence might have directed MLLAD to volunteer to the KGB in New York in order to achieve two objectives: (1) to identify the individual KGB officers responsible for espionage activities against the American atomic-weapons program and (2) to pass disinformation to the KGB. Disinformation appears plausible but is, in fact, false; it is what we saw Heydrich do to Stalin in chapter 2. The purpose of passing disinformation to the KGB would have been to deceive the Soviet atomic-weapons scientists to expend time and resources on technical blind alleys. Specifically, was plutonium really a promising alternative to uranium, or was it just an American counterintelligence ploy? The Soviet KGB has its own long and honored tradition of successful disinformation operations against western intelligence agencies; Sudoplatov suspected that MLLAD might be an American disinformation operation directed against the KGB.

Until the KGB was confident that MLLAD was a trustworthy spy and not an American disinformation agent, they refused to introduce him to a real illegal/NOC officer from the KGB. Instead, Yatskov asked MLLAD's best friend, STAR, if he would be willing to serve as the KGB's courier to MLLAD in New Mexico. STAR said that MLLAD had already asked him the same thing and that he had agreed to do so. STAR said that he and MLLAD had even worked out a simple code for sending brief messages to each other that would pass the scrutiny of the military censors at Los Alamos.

For two total amateurs, MLLAD and STAR had worked out an elegantly simple clandestine communications plan. They both purchased identical editions of Walt Whitman's twelve-poem masterpiece, *Leaves of Grass*, which they used as a simple book code to fix the date of a meeting. Specifically, MLLAD would mail a letter through the military censors to STAR in which he would quote a passage from a page in the book. The passage would correspond to a specific verse of a specific poem in their shared edition of Whitman's masterpiece. The number of that verse, one through thirty-one, would represent the day of the meeting. The number of the specific poem, one through twelve, would represent the month of the meeting. In March 1945, MLLAD evidently sent a letter to STAR quoting verse six, "The solitary guest from Alabama" of poem five, "Sea Drift," indicating a meeting for May 6.[10]

During their October meetings in New York, MLLAD and STAR agreed that they would meet next in Albuquerque. MLLAD would stay at the grand Alvarado Hotel, adjacent to the train station. STAR would stay nearby in a hotel adjacent to the Albuquerque bus terminal. They designated an easy-to-remember time, probably at noon sharp. They also designated an easy-to-remember location, First and Central.[11]

Given the highly technical nature of the information MLLAD wanted to pass, it had to be written down. Because it was top secret, it also had to be hidden from casual view. So MLLAD used a milk-based solution as a homemade invisible ink and wrote his information on the reverse side of a piece of paper that had writing in normal ink on the front.[12]

For his part, STAR needed a cover story for traveling from New York to Albuquerque during wartime. The story he developed was that he was considering enrolling in anthropology at the University of New Mexico. Prior to his trip, he reviewed the UNM course catalogue and even arranged to attend a few classes while in Albuquerque. It was lucky STAR prepared so well, because he was grilled on his arrival at the Albuquerque bus terminal by counterintelligence officers suspicious of a young, single man traveling in the middle of the war. His story was helped by adding the truth that he was exempted from military service due to a birth defect involving his left hand.

Since STAR really was MLLAD's best friend, they did not need a recognition code phrase or a cover story to explain their relationship. They could even conduct their meeting in a public venue like a café. Although their clandestine tradecraft was amateurish, everything worked well enough.

MLLAD had been part of a two-man team that had developed a method to precisely measure the fission cross-section of uranium-235. This measurement was crucial to determining the precise critical mass of U-235 needed for the simple gun-type atomic bomb eventually used over Hiroshima. Subsequently, MLLAD had also helped determine that the use of plutonium in a gun-type design would not work. Thus, in February 1945, he became involved in work to use plutonium in an implosion design. This plutonium-based design was technically more complicated than the gun-type design but far more effective and promising for future weapons development. MLLAD was in a position to provide this critically important information to the Soviets, and from the effusive KGB reaction to the information, we must assume that he did.[13]

We know STAR returned to New York City promptly after his meeting in Albuquerque with MLLAD because STAR passed the information to Yatskov in New York on Friday, May 11. Yatskov was pleased with the quality of the detailed information provided but irritated by the milk-based invisible ink. He complained that developing MLLAD's homemade secret ink just took too much time.[14]

STAR also passed information to Yatskov about another matter that was of deep security concern to KGB headquarters. During the May 6 meeting in Albuquerque, MLLAD admitted that he had revealed to a trusted friend working at Los Alamos that he had taken steps to insure that America's war ally, the Soviet Union, was kept informed about America's development of the atomic bomb. In other words, MLLAD had told someone who was a stranger to the KGB that he, MLLAD, was a KGB spy![15]

According to a July 5 cable from KGB headquarters to the KGB office in New York City in July, MLLAD's trusted friend appears to have been Harvard professor Roy Glauber.[16] Glauber never reported any such incident to Los Alamos counterintelligence and, during postwar interviews with the FBI, denied that any such conversation had ever happened. Had Glauber reported what he allegedly knew, history might have turned out quite differently. Hall (MLLAD) might have been executed for atomic espionage instead of Julius and Ethel Rosenberg. In any case, the cable from KGB headquarters severely reprimanded Anatoli Yatskov for "completely unsatisfactory" work in training MLLAD in the discipline of clandestine operations.

Suggestions for Further Reading

1. *Larger than Life: New Mexico in the Twentieth Century*, Ferenc Szasz. University of New Mexico Press, 2006. Chapter 2, "J. Robert Oppenheimer and the State of New Mexico: A Reciprocal Relationship," provides wonderful insight into Oppenheimer's love for the Land of Enchantment. Part Three, "Atomic New Mexico," contains three additional chapters on New Mexico as the home of the atomic age.

2. *The Making of the Atomic Bomb*, Richard Rhodes. Simon and Schuster, 1986. This Pulitzer Prize–winning book provides a definitive technical history of the Manhattan Project and its scientific origins. Somewhat daunting for a general reader, it focuses on the science and does not address the topic of atomic espionage.

3. *The Nuclear Express: A Political History of the Bomb and Its Proliferation*, Thomas Reed and Danny Stillman. Zenith Press, 2009. Essential reading for any citizen interested in a balanced understanding of nuclear-proliferation issues from the 1940s through the present day. More accessible to a general reader than Rhodes's *Making of the Atomic Bomb*. Pages 8–18 provide an excellent primer on the then-top-secret technical challenges that faced Los Alamos scientists in 1944–1945, including the differences between the Hiroshima gun-type bomb and the Nagasaki implosion device.

4. *Bombshell: The Secret Story of America's Unknown Atomic Spy Conspiracy*, Joseph Albright and Marcia Kunstel. Random House, 1997. An excellent book that details the atomic espionage of Ted Hall (MLLAD). The book includes a copy of the VENONA transcript, which in 1950 identified Hall to the FBI as a KGB atomic spy. The VENONA transcript is based on a November 1944 KGB report that provides the true names of Hall and his friend Saville Sax (STAR) and describes their initial contacts with the KGB in New York City in late October 1944. Chapters 13 and 14 get the timing of Sax's trip to Albuquerque wrong, however; it was not in December 1944, as estimated by Albright and Kunstel, but May 1945, as established by the subsequent work of Weinstein and Vassiliev published in *The Haunted Wood*.

5. *Brotherhood of the Bomb: The Tangled Lives of Robert Oppenheimer, Ernst Lawrence, and Edward Teller*. Gregg Herken. Henry Holt and Company, 2002. A rich human history of the three physicists who were most prominent in the creation of the nuclear era. The book provides a great feel for Oppenheimer as a morally complex and imperfect human being who, nonetheless, remained deeply loyal to the United States.

Fig. 4. (A) 56 East San Francisco Street, Santa Fe in 2009 (above, photo by author) and (B) circa the 1920s (below, courtesy of the Palace of the Governors, MNM/DCA, negative #014123).

Fig. 5. (A and B) The hidden back entrance to Trotsky's Häagen-Dazs (photos by author).

Fig. 6. (A) The present-day Alvarado Transportation Center at First and Central in Albuquerque (above, photo by author); (B) the old Alvarado Train Depot and Hotel, circa 1903 (below, courtesy of the Library of Congress, Negative #LC-USZ62–50691).

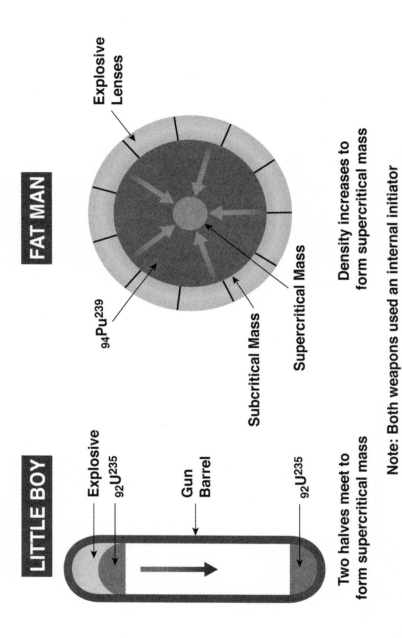

Fig. 7.
Gun- vs. implosion-type atomic designs (courtesy of Sandia National Laboratories).

Fig. 8. The "Little Boy" gun-type bomb (courtesy of Sandia National Laboratories).

Fig. 9. The "Fat Man" implosion-type bomb (courtesy of Sandia National Laboratories).

Fig. 10. (A) San Francisco Street and the south side of the Santa Fe Plaza, 2010 (above, photo by author); (B) San Francisco Street and the south side of the Santa Fe Plaza, circa 1943, with the Spitz Clock clearly visible at the center of the photo. The drugstore to the left is Capital Drugstore. Zook's Drugstore is just out of sight to the right of the photo (below, courtesy of the Palace of the Governors, MNM/DCA, negative #106739).

Fig. 11. (A) The Spitz Clock in 2010 and (B) plaque (photos by author).

THE SPITZ CLOCK

The Spitz Jewelry Store was established
on the Plaza in 1881, and a clock,
without works, was placed in front of
the store to advertise the wares offered.
Near the turn of the century, this "clock"
was replaced by a functioning sidewalk clock
which stood until 1915, when it was
knocked down by one of the first
motor trucks in Santa Fe. The third
Spitz Clock, standing here, was purchased
second-hand by Salamon Spitz in 1916
and was brought to Santa Fe from
Kansas City. It stood in front of the
Spitz Jewelry Store until the Plaza's
south portal was built in 1967. The clock was
donated to the citizens of Santa Fe by
Bernard Spitz, and was erected on this site
in June of 1974.

Fig. 12. (A) Front view of 109 East Palace Avenue and (B) commemorative plaque, 2010 (photos by author).

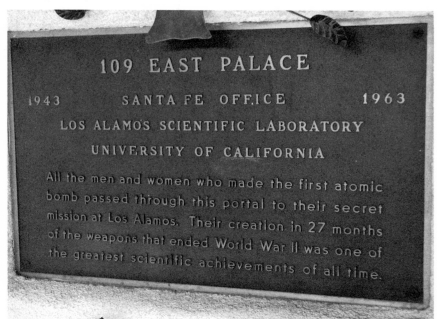

109 EAST PALACE

1943   SANTA FE OFFICE   1963

LOS ALAMOS SCIENTIFIC LABORATORY

UNIVERSITY OF CALIFORNIA

All the men and women who made the first atomic bomb passed through this portal to their secret mission at Los Alamos. Their creation in 27 months of the weapons that ended World War II was one of the greatest scientific achievements of all time.

Fig. 13. (A) The Paseo de Peralta Bridge, 2010 (above, photo by author); (B) the Castillo Bridge or possibly the adjacent Don Gaspar Bridge, circa 1930 (below, courtesy of Palace of the Governors, MNM/DCA, negative #155682).

Fig. 14. (A) View east, up Alameda Street toward where Gold waited at the bridge (above); (B) view west, down Alameda Street from where Fuchs approached (below, photos by author).

Fig. 15. (A) The house at 209 North High Street, Albuquerque, and (B) Room 4, 2010; the desk with the TV is the one that David Greenglass used to make his atomic sketches (courtesy of Steve and Kara Grant of the Spy House Bed and Breakfast).

Fig. 16. (A) The main entrance to the University of New Mexico, Central Avenue and Yale Street, 2010 (above); (B) the Scottish Rite Temple in Santa Fe, 2010 (below, photos by author).

Fig. 17. (A) The New Mexico sunset at 108 Verano Loop, Eldorado, 2010 (above); (B) Geronimo's on Canyon Road, 2010; the Howards sat at the window behind the birch trees (below, photos by author).

Fig. 18. (A–C) The author's wife in her blue Prius executes Mary's "reverse" from Camino del Monte Sol onto Acequia Madre Street, 2010 (photos by author).

Fig. 19. (A) The Y intersection of Garcia Street and Camino Corrales, Santa Fe, viewed from the northwest (above) and (B) from the southeast (below); note the 25 MPH sign, where Howard rolled out of the car (photos by author).

Fig. 20. (A) Car disappearing around the "Y" intersection (above); (B) note that you cannot see the 25 MPH sign (below, photos by author).

Fig. 21. (A) 80 Barcelona Avenue, White Rock, New Mexico, 2010 (above); (B) the Santa
Fe County Correction Center on Cerrillos Road (below, photos by author).

4 The Cold War Begins
Santa Fe, June 2, 1945

WHERE: Paseo de Peralta Bridge at the intersection of Paseo de Peralta and East Alameda Street. In 1940, the bridge here was called the Castillo Bridge, and the intersection was slightly to the west of the present-day intersection.

WHAT: On Saturday, June 2, 1945, at 4:00 in the afternoon, atomic spy Klaus Fuchs (code-named CHARLES) passed the detailed designs of America's atomic bombs to KGB operative Harry Gold (ARNO). This meeting, which took at most thirty minutes, resulted in the single greatest intelligence coup in KGB history. Gold delivered this information to KGB officer Anatoli Yatskov on June 11 in New York City.[1]

Although Soviet scientists were pleased with the information provided by the KGB's new spy MLLAD, General Sudoplatov, an experienced disinformation specialist himself, still wanted independent confirmation from a proven KGB source. He did not have to wait long to receive it and much more from the long-standing and trusted KGB source, CHARLES.

In August 1941, CHARLES had volunteered to spy for Soviet intelligence in response to Nazi Germany's invasion of the Soviet Union the previous June.[2] At the time, he was working at Birmingham University in England as a protégé of the German Jewish physicist

Rudolph Peierls. Peierls and his colleague Otto Frisch had been among the world's first scientists to recognize that a critical mass of U-235 could be used to make a simple atomic bomb. Their work was the basis for the war-strapped British government's decision in mid-1941 to finance a full-scale research program on how to build such a bomb. In turn, CHARLES provided secret information to the KGB about the British research program, which contributed to the KGB chief Lavrenti Beria's March 1942 recommendation to Stalin that the Soviet government establish its own program for atomic-weapons research. Stalin agreed to that in the fall of 1942.

In December 1943, the British government assigned Peierls and his protégé CHARLES to New York City to work with Harold Urey of Columbia University on an industrial-scale approach for separating scarce uranium-235 from the more plentiful, but unusable, uranium-238 isotope. This work was subsequently used as the basis for the uranium-235 separation-and-enrichment plant at Oak Ridge, Tennessee.

In New York, the KGB assigned a NOC officer code-named ARNO to meet clandestinely with CHARLES. ARNO, in turn, passed the secret information to KGB officer Anatoli Yatskov, who was officially assigned to the Soviet Consulate. Agent CHARLES first met NOC ARNO on February 5, 1944, at a preselected site on Henry Street on Manhattan's Lower East Side. For the next five months, they met on a monthly basis at different locations around New York City. In August, Peierls and CHARLES were abruptly assigned to Los Alamos for the specific purpose of helping the Americans figure out how to use plutonium in an implosion-type atomic bomb.

CHARLES left New York so abruptly that he had no opportunity to inform ARNO. For seven months, CHARLES and ARNO were totally out of contact. They only succeeded in reestablishing contact on February 21, 1945, in Boston, where CHARLES was given a short vacation from Los Alamos to visit his sister.[3]

During the February 1945 meeting in Boston, CHARLES confirmed what MLLAD had initially indicated to the KGB the previous October: the Americans were working on not one, but two designs for an atomic bomb. The gun-type design that used uranium-235 was simple. All that was necessary was to create a critical mass of U-235 by "shooting" one subcritical mass into another subcritical mass; hence the term "gun-type." The problem with the design was that it required a very large critical mass of U-235. At the time, American production of that isotope was quite limited. The key intelligence question for the KGB, then, was whether the Americans could produce sufficient U-235 to build a gun-type bomb before World War II ended for other reasons.

CHARLES explained to ARNO that plutonium was more promising than U-235 because (1) the critical mass of plutonium required for a bomb was much smaller, and (2) American production of plutonium was much higher. However, because plutonium would detonate prematurely in a gun-type design, scientists at Los Alamos had determined to use plutonium in an implosion-type atomic weapon. KGB–New York immediately sent a summary of this important information to Moscow via secret cable. However, the full details did not reach Russian atomic scientists until April 7, so the details were not included in the KGB's February 28 update report to Stalin (see the Chronology of Atomic Espionage).

During that February meeting in Boston, CHARLES and his KGB contact, ARNO, agreed that their next meeting would be held in Santa Fe, New Mexico, at 4:00 p.m. on Saturday, June 2, 1945. The first Saturday of each month was the only day that CHARLES was allowed to leave Los Alamos and spend time relaxing and shopping in Santa Fe. CHARLES provided ARNO a map of Santa Fe, indicating their pre-arranged meeting site at the Castillo Bridge. (Today the Castillo Bridge has been replaced by the Paseo de Peralta Bridge, located slightly to the east.)

As with STAR, ARNO needed a cover story—an ostensible reason for traveling all the way from New York City to New Mexico. ARNO's cover story was that he had respiratory problems. Since the 1930s, New Mexico, and in particular Santa Fe, had been a popular destination for Americans from the East Coast suffering from asthma, TB, emphysema, or other respiratory problems. The clear, high-desert air provided relief from the soot-filled air of New York and other big cities.

Based on STAR's grilling by officials at the Albuquerque bus terminal, however, Anatoli Yatskov felt that ARNO needed to enhance his cover story. This was not just wartime, when a man traveling by himself anywhere in the United States would draw the immediate attention of American counterintelligence. This was wartime New Mexico, which, in 1945, probably had the highest per-capita presence of counterintelligence officers of anywhere in the United States, all responsible for protecting America's top-secret atomic-bomb program sitting on the Los Alamos mesa. ARNO could not afford to draw any attention to himself.

To insure his anonymity, NOC ARNO cleverly invited his mother, who had no idea of the real purpose of the trip, to accompany him to New Mexico. He knew that Americans—even suspicious American counterintelligence officers—always trust somebody traveling with and taking care of their aged mother.[4]

Traveling by train from New York via Chicago, ARNO and his mother arrived in Albuquerque. Around noon on Saturday, June 2, ARNO, by himself, took a bus to the old Santa Fe bus station, then located at 130 Water Street. Today the same building is home to the Golden Adobe and other retail shops.

Following instructions from CHARLES, ARNO synchronized his watch with the large sidewalk clock that stood on the south side of the Santa Fe Plaza in front of the Spitz Jewelry Store. This very same Spitz clock was moved to the northwest corner of the plaza in 1974 and remains there today.[5]

As he walked from the bus station up Don Gaspar Avenue to San Francisco Street and then to the Spitz clock, ARNO would have passed directly in front of Zook's Drugstore (see chapter 2). Whether he stopped there to kill some time, have a soft drink at the drugstore fountain, or perhaps have a word or two with Katie Zook will be a subject of chapter 9.

That morning, CHARLES had attended a technical colloquium at Los Alamos. Then, he hopped into his dilapidated Buick and drove down to Santa Fe. Typically, he would have checked into the secret Los Alamos administrative office in Santa Fe, located at 109 East Palace Avenue, just northeast of the plaza. (Today these same offices form part of the delightful Rainbow Man Gallery at 107 East Palace Avenue.) Then he would have walked down to the plaza and synchronized his own watch with the Spitz clock.

With their watches properly synchronized, ARNO was on time and in place at the northwest end of what is now the Paseo de Peralta Bridge at 4:00 p.m. Driving up Alameda Street from the west, CHARLES arrived a few minutes later. From his position at the bridge, ARNO had a long, full view eastward down the street, so he could verify that nobody was following CHARLES.

Once he saw ARNO give the all-clear signal, CHARLES parked the car just east of the intersection and joined ARNO on the bridge. The two then had a short meeting to discuss security and administrative matters, including when they would meet next (September 19 at 6:00 p.m. in Santa Fe near the Scottish Rite Temple). Then they took a short drive back to the bus station.

Just before he dropped ARNO off, CHARLES handed him a large package of information.[6] In it were comprehensive technical details of Fat Man, the plutonium-based implosion bomb that would be used at Nagasaki and the critical piece of information that the Americans felt no need to test Little Boy, the gun-type bomb that would be used at Hiroshima. (The Americans knew Little Boy would work; and besides, they had enough weapons-grade U-235 for only one bomb.) The information advised that a test of the Nagasaki implosion design would take place at the Trinity site on or about July 10, only five weeks away; if the test was successful, the Americans had sufficient plutonium to produce at least five more bombs for use against Japan that year.

On the night of June 11, ARNO turned this information over to Anatoli Yatskov during a brief, clandestine encounter in New York City. Two days later, Yatskov sent a telegram to KGB headquarters summarizing the key points. The full details were sent to Moscow under armed guard via Soviet diplomatic pouch. On July 2, the KGB gave a detailed technical report to the team of scientists leading the Soviet research program for an atomic bomb.[7]

General Sudoplatov and the rest of the KGB were ecstatic about the information CHARLES provided. It independently confirmed the reliability of MLLAD's report four weeks earlier. Not only was the information much more detailed, it included the critically impor-tant technical data about the Urchin initiator used to trigger the implosion-design bomb. These details and information were key to the Soviet's postwar efforts to build their own arsenal of Fat Man atomic bombs.

Josef Stalin was pleased as well. By mid-June 1945, Stalin could predict with confidence that America's war with Japan would probably end abruptly in late July or early August. So, if Stalin wanted to maximize Soviet territorial gains in Manchuria and northern Korea, which he certainly did want to do, then he would need to renounce the Soviet-Japanese nonaggression pact of April

1941 and hustle tired Soviet troops from their victory celebrations in Germany eastward to Asia as quickly as possible.

President Harry Truman and Secretary of State Jimmy Byrnes, in contrast, hoped that the U.S. bombs would prompt Tokyo to surrender before the Soviets were in position to enter the war against the Japanese and thereby deny the Soviets a share of the war spoils in Asia. To avoid alerting Stalin to the significance of the new weapons during the Potsdam Conference, Truman limited his comments on July 24 to a casual reference about a "new weapon of unusual destructive force." He revealed no details of the successful test of Fat Man at Trinity the previous week.[8]

Thanks in large part to CHARLES and the other KGB atomic spies, however, Stalin got the better of Truman. The Soviets declared war against the Japanese on August 8, just two days after Hiroshima, and immediately moved troops into Manchuria and northern Korea. The Red Army took nearly two million Japanese soldiers prisoner and used them as forced labor in the Soviet postwar recovery effort. More than three hundred thousand of these prisoners never returned from captivity in Siberia, and repatriation of those that did return was not completed until 1949.[9] How different their fate might have been but for KGB atomic espionage.

Suggestions for Further Reading

1. *Dark Sun: The Making of the Hydrogen Bomb,* Richard Rhodes. Simon and Schuster, 1995. A superbly detailed and comprehensive work that includes excellent sections related to the espionage of David Greenglass and the Rosenbergs, as well as Klaus Fuchs. The only weakness is that the book was published before Ted Hall was publicly identified as MLLAD.

2. *Klaus Fuchs: Atom Spy,* Robert Chadwell Williams. Harvard University Press, 1987. Published before the fall of the Berlin Wall and the declassification of VENONA, the book is somewhat dated. It does include the confessions of Klaus Fuchs (CHARLES) to Britain's MI-5 and Harry Gold (ARNO) to the FBI.

3. *Klaus Fuchs: A Biography,* Norman Moss. St. Martin's Press, 1987. Another excellent biography of Fuchs but published before the fall of the Berlin Wall and the declassification of VENONA.

4. *Breakdown: How the Secret of the Atomic Bomb Was Stolen During World War II,* Richard Melzer. Sunstone Press, 2000. A delightful little book that first stimulated my interest in the espionage history of New Mexico.

5. *Building the Bombs: A History of the Nuclear Weapons Complex,* Charles Loeber. Sandia National Laboratories, 2003. This excellent history is accessible and understandable to general readers.

5 The Cold War Begins
Albuquerque, June 3, 1945

WHERE: The Freeman boarding house, 209 North High Street. Today this is the Spy House, a charming bed and breakfast where spy buffs can spend a history-packed evening. (For information, call 505-842-0223.)

WHAT: In Room 4, on the second floor at the back of the house, on this day, KGB operative Harry Gold (ARNO) met briefly twice with atomic spy David Greenglass (BUMBLEBEE) and his wife, Ruth (WASP). The only occasion Gold met the Greenglass couple, it turned into one of the great disasters in KGB history, leading to the identification of David's sister and brother-in-law, Ethel and Julius Rosenberg.

After his June 2 meeting with CHARLES in Santa Fe, ARNO took the bus back to Albuquerque. The next morning, against all his instincts as a clandestine operative, ARNO walked over to the Freeman boarding house at 209 North High Street to try to make contact with another KGB atomic spy, code-named BUMBLEBEE, a man he had never met.[1]

ARNO had objected strenuously when his KGB boss, Anatoli Yatskov, had ordered him to make contact with BUMBLEBEE in Albuquerque. It was bad clandestine tradecraft. For security purposes, KGB rules dictated that a NOC meet only with one agent. NOC ANTENNA (Julius Rosenberg), not NOC ARNO (Harry Gold), was assigned to meet with agent BUMBLEBEE (David Greenglass). ARNO did not even know the true names of ANTENNA or BUMBLEBEE, and good tradecraft dictated that it should remain that way.

When ARNO objected to the assignment, Yatskov reminded him that the dictates of Josef Stalin trumped KGB tradecraft and that Stalin was demanding results. The KGB feared that ANTENNA (Rosenberg) had come to the attention of American counterintelligence in New York. If that was true, ANTENNA had no plausible cover story for traveling to New Mexico to meet BUMBLEBEE. So Stalin's man at the KGB, General Sudoplatov, directed that ARNO meet BUMBLEBEE instead. Given Stalin's simple managerial philosophy—obey or die —neither Yatskov nor Sudoplatov were inclined to question Stalin's judgment on this or any other matter.

In the summer of 1945, David Greenglass was a twenty-three-year-old Army sergeant assigned to Los Alamos as a machinist. The son of a Russian immigrant, he had grown up in poverty in an unheated tenement on Manhattan's Lower East Side. He had two older brothers and an older sister, Ethel. Even as a teenager, Ethel was engaged in left-wing, Depression-era politics. In 1939, at age twenty-four, Ethel married a twenty-one-year-old member of the Young Communist League named Julius Rosenberg.

Greenglass and Ruth, his nineteen-year-old childhood sweetheart, had also participated in the Young Communist League. In November 1942, David and Ruth married. Five months later, Greenglass was drafted into the Army and assigned as a machinist, first at Fort Ord, California, later at the Mississippi Ordnance Plant in Jackson, Mississippi; Ruth remained in New York. In July 1944, Greenglass was assigned briefly to the secret installation at Oak Ridge, Tennessee, which was part of the so-called "Manhattan Engineer District." In a letter to him, Ruth wrote that Julius (David's brother-in-law) somehow knew all about the secret work that was underway at Oak Ridge.[2]

Almost immediately, Greenglass was reassigned to an even more secret installation somewhere near Santa Fe. En route to New Mexico, David sent Ruth a letter warning that his work there would be so secret that she should take care not to mention anything politically sensitive again in future letters that might draw the attention of the installation censors. On August 5, Greenglass arrived at Los Alamos. On September 21, 1944, KGB–New York asked

Moscow's permission to have ANTENNA (Julius Rosenberg) recruit Greenglass as an atomic spy and to use Ruth as a courier from New York City to New Mexico. Two weeks later, Moscow granted KGB–New York permission to proceed as proposed, recruiting Greenglass (code-named BUMBLEBEE) and his wife, Ruth, code-named WASP.[3]

On November 4, BUMBLEBEE sent a cryptic letter to WASP in New York, alerting her to his willingness to cooperate with Julius and his "friends." Less than two weeks later, WASP had dinner with Julius and Ethel. Julius spoke of the tremendous sacrifices of the Soviet people in combating the Nazis as the reason BUMBLEBEE should share critically important defense secrets with Moscow. When WASP expressed concern about the risks involved, Ethel stressed that her brother, BUMBLEBEE, would want to help.[4]

Using KGB money supplied by ANTENNA (Julius), WASP traveled to Albuquerque, ostensibly to celebrate her second wedding anniversary with BUMBLEBEE. She arrived on Sunday, November 26; BUMBLEBEE received a short furlough from Los Alamos and joined her at the Franciscan Hotel in Albuquerque Tuesday night through Sunday afternoon, December 3. As Ethel had predicted, BUMBLE-BEE readily agreed to cooperate with ANTENNA and the KGB. KGB–New York so advised Moscow in a cable sent December 16, 1944.

On New Year's Day 1945, BUMBLEBEE arrived in New York City on family leave to visit his wife, WASP. His brother-in-law, ANTENNA, showed up promptly to learn the latest news from Los Alamos. ANTENNA explained his understanding that an atomic explosion was created by shooting one subcritical mass of radioactive material into another subcritical mass, creating an explosive critical mass. He asked BUMBLEBEE what part of the bomb he was working on. To ANTENNA's surprise, BUMBLEBEE responded that the bomb he was working on did not operate in that way. Rather, BUMBLEBEE said, he was working on a design that would use explosive charges to compress the radioactive material into a critical mass, i.e., he was working on an implosion-type atomic bomb. This was a totally new concept to ANTENNA.

ANTENNA immediately communicated this news to his KGB contact in New York, Alexander Feklisov. He, in turn, arranged an urgent clandestine meeting between BUMBLEBEE and an unknown Soviet technical expert who would ask follow-up questions about this implosion design. Besides the new technical data about the design of the bomb, the KGB–New York placed great importance on this information because it was evidently the first confirmation of the report from their new source MLLAD (Ted Hall) two months earlier. BUMBLEBEE's information, while not conclusive proof that MLLAD was a real spy rather than an American disinformation agent, was a positive indication that MLLAD might be trustworthy.

On January 20, BUMBLEBEE reported back to Los Alamos. In February, his wife, WASP, again using KGB money supplied by ANTENNA, moved to Albuquerque and rented Room 4 in the Freeman boarding house. As a low-level machinist, BUMBLEBEE had fewer work responsibilities than physicists like CHARLES and MLLAD and was authorized to leave Los Alamos each weekend for conjugal visits with WASP in Albuquerque.

KGB officer Yatskov directed ARNO to try to make contact with BUMBLEBEE at his boarding house on Sunday morning. He advised ARNO to introduce himself as a friend of Julius so that BUMBLEBEE would know ARNO was with the KGB and not one of the many American counterintelligence agents in New Mexico. He was also to present one half of a torn Jell-O box. BUMBLEBEE would confirm his identity by producing the other half of the same Jell-O box. NOC ANTENNA and BUMBLEBEE had agreed on this Jell-O box trick during their meetings in New York in January.[5]

After they successfully identified themselves to each other, BUMBLEBEE explained that he had very limited knowledge about what was going on at Los Alamos. Counterintelligence required that everything be compartmented according to a need-to-know principle. Accordingly, BUMBLEBEE knew that he was working on an explosive lens device that would direct the force inward not outward: an implosion, not an explosion. He did not know much else about how the bomb worked.

ARNO nonetheless directed BUMBLEBEE to write out everything he knew about the device, including what it was made of and what type of explosives were being used. He also told BUMBLEBEE to draw as accurate a diagram of the device as he could, with all the dimensions. BUMBLEBEE agreed and said it would take him a few hours. ARNO left. Later that day he returned, picked up the material, and paid BUMBLEBEE five hundred dollars for his efforts. Shortly thereafter, ARNO and his mother left Albuquerque for New York, thinking that all was well.

On the night of June 11, ARNO gave Anatoli Yatskov all the atomic secrets that he had collected during his two clandestine meetings in New Mexico. The information from CHARLES (Klaus Fuchs) was invaluable in advancing the Soviets' atomic-weapons program and their planning for the end of the war against Japan. The information from BUMBLEBEE (David Greenglass) was of marginal value, especially compared to the more detailed information provided by Fuchs in June and Hall in May. Nevertheless, the five hundred dollars paid to Greenglass was more than Fuchs and Hall combined ever received from the KGB during their entire careers as Soviet spies. Most importantly for the KGB–New York officers, the meeting with BUMBLEBEE helped demonstrate to Stalin and General Sudoplatov that they were doing everything in their power to collect all the information they could about ENORMOZ, the American atomic-bomb project.

ARNO (Harry Gold) was proven correct in his objection to meeting BUMBLEBEE. Six years later, in 1951, that tradecraft mistake would result in the arrest of Julius Rosenberg (ANTENNA) and his wife, Ethel Greenglass Rosenberg. Julius and Ethel paid for this mistake with their lives in the electric chair at Sing Sing Prison in New York. (Chapter 8 reveals the chain of events that led to the unraveling of the Rosenberg case by American counterintelligence.)

Suggestions for Further Reading

1. *The Rosenberg File*, 2nd ed., Ronald Radosh and Joyce Milton. Yale University Press, 1997. Although dated, Radosh and Milton's work has stood the test of time. The lengthy introduction to the second edition details the impact of new information from VENONA and KGB sources.

2. *The Brother: The Untold Story of Atomic Spy David Greenglass and How He Sent His Sister, Ethel Rosenberg, to the Electric Chair*, Sam Roberts. Random House, 2001. A curious book that demonstrates the emotional hold of the Rosenberg/Greenglass case despite public proof beyond any doubt that Julius Rosenberg and David Greenglass were Soviet spies and their wives, Ethel Rosenberg and Ruth Greenglass, were coconspirators. The author expresses admiration that the Rosenbergs were willing to die defending their innocence (despite its being untrue) and expresses considerable contempt that the Greenglasses saved themselves by confessing the truth of their espionage activities. Roberts's attitude goes to the heart of the ethics-and-espionage conundrum; the motivation for espionage is what matters to many people, not the espionage itself.

3. *The Man Behind the Rosenbergs*, Alexander Feklisov. Enigma Books, 2004. After it had been publicly established that Julius Rosenberg was a Soviet spy and Ethel was a coconspirator, their KGB control officer confirms those facts. Feklisov, a respected and distinguished intelligence officer, goes on to suggest that all civilized people, including Americans, should consider the Rosenbergs heroes. Decorated himself as a Hero of the Soviet Union, Feklisov also criticizes his own KGB for exploiting the Rosenbergs as propaganda pawns rather than negotiating to rescue them.

6 The First Act Ends
Albuquerque, August 5, 1945

WHERE: The University of New Mexico's main entrance at Central Avenue and Yale Street.

WHAT: In the vicinity of this intersection, Harvard graduate and atomic spy Ted Hall (MLLAD) met KGB operative Lona Cohen (LESLIE). Hall provided Cohen technical details about the successful test of America's atomic bomb, which he had witnessed on July 16 at the Trinity test site. At about the same moment that Hall was meeting Cohen (Monday, August 6, Japan time), the Americans dropped the Little Boy atomic bomb on Hiroshima. This was the last time Hall would meet the KGB in New Mexico.[1]

KGB General Sudoplatov had finally accepted MLLAD as a bona fide spy in mid-June 1945, after the report from trusted KGB agent CHARLES confirmed the accuracy of an earlier report by MLLAD. KGB–New York therefore decided that it was safe to replace the amateur STAR (Saville Sax) with a professional KGB operative as their courier to MLLAD in New Mexico. Anatoli Yatskov selected a female NOC officer code-named LESLIE for the job.

Since the KGB was expecting the Trinity atomic test to take place on or about July 10, they evidently hoped to arrange another meeting with MLLAD on Sunday, July 15. To set that meeting date, STAR would have sent a letter to MLLAD sometime in mid-June. Again using Whitman's *Leaves of Grass* as a "book code," STAR would have asked MLLAD's opinion of the verse "Vigil strange I kept on the field one night" from the "Drum-Taps" poem. That would correspond to verse 15 of poem 7, thus indicating a meeting on July 15. STAR would also have indicated that he, personally, did not like the specified passage but that he had a close woman friend named LESLIE who did like that verse very much indeed.

As ARNO had done to meet CHARLES in June, LESLIE traveled by train from New York, using the cover story that she was seeking a cure for respiratory problems. Due to the heavy presence of American counterintelligence in Albuquerque, however, LESLIE decided that it would be safer to stay in the small, hot-springs town of Las Vegas, on the railway line 120 miles northeast of Albuquerque. She went to Albuquerque on Sunday, July 15 under the guise of a sightseeing excursion and proceeded to the predesignated meeting site on the University of New Mexico campus. When MLLAD failed to appear, LESLIE returned to Las Vegas the same evening. She tried again the following Sunday and a third time on Sunday, July 29, but still no MLLAD. She decided to try one final time on Sunday, August 5, and one way or the other, would return to New York the next day.

The fourth time was the charm—MLLAD showed up. Yatskov had shown LESLIE a picture of MLLAD, so she recognized him. They walked around the UNM campus for about thirty minutes. He wanted to talk about the Trinity test. Pursuant to the KGB reprimand of Yatskov, she wanted to talk about the security implications of MLLAD's inadvisable revelation to Professor Glauber. MLLAD gave LESLIE five or six pages of technical data, presumably related to the results of the Trinity test. LESLIE concealed them in the bottom of her tissue box. She returned to New York City and, later that week, passed the information on to Anatoli Yatskov. By then, however, the KGB didn't need the information to tell them whether the atomic bomb test had been successful; after the August 9 bombing of Nagasaki, that was no longer a secret to anybody.[2]

The meeting with LESLIE was the last clandestine meeting MLLAD ever had with the KGB in New Mexico. The Army terminated Ted Hall's top-secret security clearance in June 1946, and shortly thereafter he was honorably discharged.

After the war ended, Hall switched his interest from nuclear physics to the less-sensitive area of biophysics. After finishing his PhD at the University of Chicago, he began work as a cancer researcher at Memorial Sloan Kettering Cancer Center in New York City. In the early 1960s, he and his family immigrated to England, where he became a professor of biophysics at Cambridge University.

Hall returned to New Mexico only once, in August 1986, as the keynote speaker at the annual meeting of the Electron Microscopy Association of America. His host, a senior official in the U.S. nuclear-weapons program, was totally unwitting of Hall's then-secret history as one of the KGB's most important atomic spies. Hall wandered around the University of New Mexico campus looking for the spot of his secret meeting with LESLIE (Lona Cohen) in August 1945, but the area had changed so much he couldn't find it. During that trip to New Mexico, Los Alamos invited Hall up to the mesa for a visit, but he considered it prudent to decline.

Late in life, Hall admitted that as a young man, he had been mistaken in his understanding of the nature of the Soviet Union. However, he expressed no regret for his spying on behalf of the KBG.

Suggestions for Further Reading

1. *The Day the Sun Rose Twice: The Story of the Trinity Site Nuclear Explosion, July 16, 1945*, Ferenc Szasz. University of New Mexico Press, 1984. A bit dated, this book remains essential reading for anyone planning to visit the Trinity site on the two days each year that it is open to the general public: the first Saturday in April and the first Saturday in October.

7 The First Act Ends
Santa Fe, September 19, 1945

WHERE: The northeast corner of the intersection of Paseo de Peralta and Bishops Lodge Road, across from the Scottish Rite Temple.

WHAT: At this spot, at 6:00 in the evening, atomic spy CHARLES (Klaus Fuchs) picked up KGB operative ARNO (Harry Gold) and drove into the foothills overlooking Santa Fe. CHARLES provided ARNO technical details about the mid-July Trinity test and the early August bombings on Hiroshima and Nagasaki. CHARLES also advised ARNO about strong support among Los Alamos scientists for sharing technical information about the atomic bomb with the Soviet Union. This was the last time Fuchs would meet the KGB in New Mexico.[1]

Since the last time NOC ARNO met CHARLES, on June 2, the world had changed irrevocably. The atomic age began with the July 16 test at the Trinity Site, at which CHARLES was present. Three weeks later, Little Boy, the simple, gun-type atomic bomb, was detonated over Hiroshima, killing up to 140,000 people. Three days after that, Fat Man, the more complicated but more effective implosion device, was detonated over Nagasaki, killing up to 70,000 people. The first thing CHARLES asked ARNO after picking him up on the evening of September 19 was "Were you impressed?" ARNO replied that he was impressed but horrified.[2]

In June, when he planned the meeting with ARNO, CHARLES had known that, for better or worse, the world would be different in September. So he felt comfortable setting a meeting date for a Wednesday rather than the normal, weekend rendezvous. He chose a time two hours later, however, so that he and ARNO could meet under the cover of darkness. This was fine for the meeting itself, but the long bus ride back to his hotel in Albuquerque made ARNO quite nervous. Once again, his mother accompanied him on the trip, and she, too, was worried about his being out so late.

Although CHARLES gave ARNO detailed technical reports about Trinity and the two Japanese cities, CHARLES was already focused on the future. He told ARNO that he would be leaving Los Alamos in a matter of weeks and be returning to England to work inside the British atomic-weapons program at Harwell. Accordingly, he and ARNO agreed to the time and place for their next meeting in London after the turn of the new year.

CHARLES advised ARNO that an influential group of scientists at Los Alamos, led by Nils Bohr, was lobbying to share the secrets of the atomic bomb with the Soviet Union. CHARLES correctly predicted, however, that the American and British governments would reject the idea. Hence, CHARLES considered it his duty to continue sharing this information with Moscow via clandestine KGB channels.[3]

This was the last time CHARLES (Klaus Fuchs) met with the KGB in New Mexico. He never returned to the state.

When Fuchs was exposed as a Soviet spy in 1950, his colleagues at Los Alamos were stunned. They thought all spies were scum, but Fuchs was such a likeable, hard working, decent person. His closest colleagues never could have imagined he would betray them and their work. At his trial, Fuchs himself explained that a "controlled schizophrenia" had allowed him to make true friendships and conduct sincere personal relationships all while leading a secret, double life as a Soviet spy. He kept two separate and distinct compartments in his mind: one as a spy, the other as a respected colleague and sincere personal friend. As complicated as it sounded, he was honest in both of those compartments.

8 Some Guilty, Some Not
KGB Atomic Spies in New Mexico

WHAT: VENONA was the code name for a top-secret U.S. counter-intelligence program that broke the KGB communication code used during 1944–1945. It was as a result of VENONA that American counterintelligence knew for a fact that Julius Rosenberg, Klaus Fuchs, David Greenglass, Ted Hall, Saville Sax, and Harry Gold were KGB spies. American counterintelligence also had compelling evidence that J. Robert Oppenheimer was not a KGB spy. Although the KGB learned of VENONA in 1949, the successful code-breaking program was unfortunately kept secret from the American public until 1995.[1]

After meeting secretly with NOC ARNO on June 11, Anatoli Yatskov rushed back to his KGB office in New York City. He sent the full, technical details and diagrams that ARNO had received from CHARLES and BUMBLEBEE to Moscow via diplomatic pouch under armed guard. Due to the war with Germany, it took several weeks for such diplomatic pouches to travel from New York via Great Falls, Montana, Siberia, and finally to Moscow. However, Yatskov summarized the key points of urgent interest to Stalin and General Sudoplatov in top-secret telegrams. Surprisingly, the KGB sent these telegrams directly to Moscow from the Western Union office in New York City.

Not surprisingly, patriotic Americans working in Western Union gave copies of these top-secret KGB telegrams to American counterintelligence officers working for the FBI. Counterintelligence filed all the messages but could not read them because they were encrypted. The encryption system used by the KGB was referred to as "one-time pads." As the name would suggest, one-time pads were supposed to be used only once, which made it impossible for American counterintelligence to break the code and read the encrypted telegrams.

Unfortunately for the KGB, their one-time pads were also sent from Moscow to New York via diplomatic pouch under armed guard, and likewise it took several weeks for these diplomatic pouches to make the trip. Because of these delays, the KGB occasionally had to use their one-time pads more than once . . . sometimes twice . . . sometimes three times . . . sometimes even four times. As soon as American counterintelligence realized this, they did their utmost to make sure that Soviet diplomatic pouches and their armed guards ran into more "unexpected" delays on their way from Moscow, via Siberia and Montana, to the Western Union office in New York City. When the KGB used their one-time pads more than once, American counterintelligence was able to break the code and begin reading the top-secret KGB telegrams to General Sudoplatov and Josef Stalin provided by those patriotic Americans working in the Western Union office.

Decrypting the KGB telegrams was still a long, arduous task, because in the late 1940s, computers had only just been invented and were still primitive. By 1949, however, American counterintelligence had succeeded in determining the code names of the four KGB spies working in the Los Alamos laboratory during 1944–1945: CHARLES, BUMBLEBEE, MLLAD, and PERSEUS.

The next challenge was to identify the true names of those four atomic spies. Here, American counterintelligence got lucky twice. In one secret telegram, the KGB inadvertently used the actual name of CHARLES—Klaus Fuchs—instead of his code name. In another secret telegram, the KGB in New York used true names to report its very first contacts with Ted Hall and his friend Saville Sax. Only subsequently was Hall code-named MLLAD and Sax, STAR.

Upon deeper investigation, American counterintelligence learned that Klaus Fuchs was a young German communist who had fled Hitler's Gestapo in 1933 and settled in England. A brilliant physicist, Fuchs completed his doctoral studies at the University of Bristol in 1936 at the age of twenty-five. He became a naturalized British citizen in 1942. Although his communist background was known to the British authorities, they granted Fuchs a top-secret security clearance for two reasons. First, the British government needed his scientific talent for its atomic effort. Second, Fuchs had won the trust and confidence of British intelligence by helping it monitor the progress of the German atomic effort. What the British did not realize was that Fuchs was simultaneously reporting everything he knew about both the British and German programs to Soviet intelligence.[2]

By the time American code breakers identified him in 1949, Fuchs was back living in England and working as the head of the theoretical-physics division of Britain's own atomic-weapons laboratory at Harwell. American counterintelligence informed the senior representative of British counterintelligence at the British Embassy in Washington, D.C., a man named Kim Philby. Like Fuchs, Philby was a long-time spy for the Soviet KGB!

Philby warned the KGB that Fuchs was about to be arrested, but the KGB decided not to warn Fuchs. They evidently calculated that warning Fuchs would put Philby in danger. So the KGB simply let the chips fall where they may.[3]

In 1950, British counterintelligence confronted Fuchs but took care to do so without revealing anything about the top-secret VENONA program. Fuchs quickly confessed. In fact, he was rather proud of what he had done. After his confession, British counterintelligence very politely offered him a choice: either he cooperate with counterintelligence or he would be put to death. Fuchs chose cooperation. Cooperation meant that Fuchs was obliged to identify his KGB contact, the NOC code-named ARNO. Since ARNO was an American with the true name of Harry Gold, British counterintelligence directed their man in Washington, Philby, to inform American counterintelligence. Philby did so, but only after first informing his KGB masters.

American counterintelligence arrested Gold and offered him the same choice Fuchs had been offered. Gold, too, chose cooperation. However, Gold could not betray the identity of Fuchs, because Fuchs was the one who had betrayed the identity of Gold. So Gold identified the only other atomic spies that he knew: the couple he had met only one time, at 209 North High Street in Albuquerque, agents BUM-BLEBEE (David Greenglass) and his wife, WASP (Ruth Greenglass).

American counterintelligence arrested David and Ruth and offered them cooperation or death. Like Fuchs and Gold before them, they chose cooperation. However, the Greenglasses could not betray the identity of Gold because Gold had already betrayed their identity. So David and Ruth identified the only other atomic spy that they knew—the NOC code-named ANTENNA, David's brother-in-law, Julius Rosenberg.

Still careful to protect the secret of VENONA, American counterintelligence hoped that Julius and Ethel Rosenberg would betray the identity of other spies, including MLLAD and PERSEUS. However, Julius and Ethel refused to cooperate. They went to their deaths as true believers in the communist cause and protecting the identities of their espionage co-conspirators. Their KGB–New York contact, Aleksandr Feklisov, was deeply angered when the KGB simply abandoned the Rosenbergs rather than negotiate their release.[4]

An important point to reiterate is that American counterintelligence never needed to reveal anything about the top-secret VENONA program in open court. Fuchs's confession led to Gold's confession. Gold's confession led to the Greenglass's confession. The Rosenbergs were convicted in 1951 and sentenced to death based on the testimony from Gold and the Greenglasses.

In 1951, while the Rosenberg trial was making headlines as the "Crime of the Century," American counterintelligence confronted Ted Hall (MLLAD) and Saville Sax (STAR), again without revealing anything about the top-secret VENONA program. Hall and Sax, like Fuchs, were proud of what they had done. Unlike Fuchs, they refused to confess. They both denied everything, admitted nothing.

The FBI in Chicago simultaneously interviewed the two men for three hours but were unable to crack their stories. The FBI then interviewed Roy Glauber at Harvard, the professor to whom Hall allegedly revealed his intent to commit espionage. Glauber denied any recollection of such an admission to him by Hall. From VENONA, the FBI knew absolutely that Hall and Sax were lying, but the FBI had no evidence to present in court without revealing details from the top-secret program. The FBI was *not* willing to do that.

The FBI had tried to trap Hall and Sax by surveilling them for more than a year before calling them in for interviews. This surveillance had produced no indication that either of the men remained in continuing contact with the KGB. Moreover, since his departure from Los Alamos, Hall no longer had a security clearance.

He still had old classified information in his brain, all of which he had presumably passed to the KGB already. He did not have current access to new classified information, however. So, in late 1951, the FBI gave up on the idea of arresting and prosecuting Hall and Sax for espionage. However, the FBI would continue to monitor the activities of the two men.[5]

By coincidence perhaps, Ted Hall and his wife, Joan, drove by Sing Sing Prison on the evening of June 19, 1953, on their way to a dinner party with friends. Ted had confessed his wartime atomic-espionage activities to Joan shortly before their 1947 marriage. The confession had caused the eighteen-year-old Joan to love and admire Ted even more. Now, driving by Sing Sing just a few hours before Julius and Ethel Rosenberg were executed, they both quietly realized how deadly a game real espionage can be.

The Rosenbergs, the Greenglasses, Fuchs, and Gold were all guilty of espionage, and they all paid a price for it. Hall and Sax were equally guilty of espionage but paid little, if any, price. J. Robert Oppenheimer, by comparison, was *not* guilty of espionage but paid a considerable price nonetheless.

In 1954, Oppenheimer, referred to as the "American Prometheus" in a book by that title, was publicly humiliated by having his security clearance revoked and his loyalty to America questioned. There was no doubt about Oppenheimer's ideological flirtation with communism and his personal association with communists during the 1930s and early 1940s. General Leslie Groves, the military head of America's atomic-weapons program, knew all that before naming Oppenheimer as the scientific director of Los Alamos.

After the war, Oppenheimer made no secret of his support for some sort of international arrangement to share knowledge about atomic power. He also had moral reservations about research and development of advanced nuclear weapons hundreds of times more powerful than the Hiroshima Little Boy and the Nagasaki Fat Man bombs. Any American was free to agree or disagree with Oppenheimer on these matters of national policy. However, J. Robert Oppenheimer was not a KGB spy. Anybody with access to VENONA would have known that.

The VENONA program was top secret. There is no indication that during his presidency in 1945–1952, Harry S. Truman was *ever* briefed on what the VENONA evidence proved to American counterintelligence regarding Soviet atomic espionage in New Mexico. Josef Stalin learned all about the VENONA evidence in 1949, thanks to the KGB spy Kim Philby, but President Truman did not.[6]

In 1961, America's new president, John Kennedy, transferred control of VENONA from J. Edgar Hoover at the FBI to his trusted, personal acquaintance James Jesus Angleton, the CIA's chief of counterintelligence. Kennedy wanted to know how strong the counterintelligence case against the Rosenbergs and Oppenheimer truly was. Angleton would have had no doubt about the guilt of the Rosenbergs. Regarding Oppenheimer, however, it all depended on how he interpreted the VENONA transcripts. Angleton loved to give Delphic answers to straightforward questions, but John Kennedy was now the commander in chief, and he demanded a straightforward answer.

In 1963, Angleton was in position to report to the president that the VENONA evidence regarding Oppenheimer was not cut and dried. There was room for an honest difference in opinion. Oppenheimer did have a history of communist associations. That said, VENONA provided compelling evidence that Oppenheimer had never revealed American atomic secrets to the Soviet Union. Oppenheimer was not a KGB spy.[7]

On the basis of this counterintelligence assessment, President Kennedy made a gesture of healing in an attempt to correct a historical wrong. He awarded Oppenheimer the Enrico Fermi Medal for Distinguished Scientific Contributions to America. The Fermi Medal was presented to Oppenheimer at the White House by President Johnson less than a week after President Kennedy was assassinated in Dallas.

The controversy about Oppenheimer was stirred again in 1994, when Josef Stalin's man at the KGB, General Sudoplatov, published his astonishing memoir of his life as a KGB assassin and disinformation specialist. Although he was eighty-seven years old at the time (he would die two years later), Sudoplatov still could not resist lacing his memoir with a new dose of disinformation. Specifically, he claimed that the KGB source code-named MLLAD was the Italian scientist Bruno Pontecorvo, who later defected to the Soviet Union.

Sudoplatov also alleged that J. Robert Oppenheimer was the agent code-named STAR and had passed secret messages to the KGB via Zook's Drugstore in Santa Fe, the same drugstore that the KGB had used to support the 1940 assassination of Leon Trotsky (see chapter 2).[8]

Anybody with access to the VENONA transcripts knew that Sudoplatov's allegations were nonsense. American counterintelligence knew for a fact that MLLAD was Ted Hall and that STAR was Saville Sax. So the CIA director at the time, John Deutch, made the long-overdue decision to declassify VENONA and let the American public in on the secret.

Some American counterintelligence specialists reflexively opposed Deutch's decision. Their opposition was overcome by a simple, factual timeline of who knew what when:

* In 1945, the KGB had four spies working inside Los Alamos.
* In 1949, American counterintelligence knew from VENONA that the KGB had four spies working inside of Los Alamos in 1945.
* In 1949, the KGB knew from Kim Philby that American counterintelligence knew about their 1945 spies inside Los Alamos. Moreover, the KGB knew how American counterintelligence knew.
* In 1963, when Philby defected to Moscow, American counterintelligence knew that the KGB knew that American counterintelligence knew.

By 1963 then, the only people who cared about the truth but did not know the truth were the American public! Thirty-two years later, CIA Director Deutch decided that enough was enough. The American public not only had a right to know, they had a "need to know."

The identity of atomic spy PERSEUS has never been revealed publicly. A key question is whether PERSEUS continued to work inside Los Alamos after the war, providing the KGB with secret details on the American development of H-bombs hundreds of times more powerful than A-bombs.

In 1991, the KGB told the world that PERSEUS was a well-placed American scientist at Los Alamos who had volunteered to work for the KGB. The KGB contact for PERSEUS was an American woman, then living in Moscow, named Lona Cohen (code-named LESLIE).

We know that Cohen was the same woman who had met Ted Hall (MLLAD) on the University of New Mexico campus in Albuquerque on August 5, 1945 (see chapter 6). The KGB asserted that PERSEUS had first befriended Lona's husband and fellow KGB operative, Morris Cohen, while they were both fighting in the Spanish Civil War.[9]

Based on a partially decoded KGB telegram dated December 13, 1944, American counterintelligence had a hint that PERSEUS had recently transferred to Los Alamos, apparently from Oak Ridge.[10] This VENONA information, plus the unverifiable KGB claim that PERSEUS was a Spanish Civil War veteran, would point a possible finger at Louis Slotin.

Slotin was a Canadian physicist of Russian Jewish parents. After receiving his PhD in London, he fought in the Spanish Civil War as a member of the International Brigade of the Spanish Republic. In the early 1940s, he worked at the University of Chicago with Enrico Fermi and then at Oak Ridge. In December 1944, he transferred from Oak Ridge to Los Alamos.

Slotin died a hero in 1946 at Los Alamos when an experiment with a critical mass of plutonium went awry. Acting quickly to avoid an atomic disaster, Slotin exposed himself to a lethal dose of radiation and died an excruciating death a few days later.

An alternative explanation of the PERSEUS story is provided by Allen Weinstein and Alexander Vassiliev in their exceptional book, *The Haunted Wood*. Based on their review of classified KGB files, PERSEUS appears to have been a construction engineer, not a scientist, without direct access to important atomic secrets, and he may never even have served at Los Alamos.[11]

If either of these stories is true, then PERSEUS did not provide the KGB with secret details on American work to develop H-bombs. Of course, both stories might represent KGB disinformation, in which case we will probably never know the truth regarding the identity of PERSEUS.

Suggestions for Further Reading

1. *VENONA: Soviet Espionage and the American Response, 1939–1957*, Robert Louis Benson and Michael Warner, eds. National Security Agency/Central Intelligence Agency, 1996. Declassification of VENONA has fundamentally changed the public's understanding of American Cold War history. This remarkable book includes the original texts of the most important decoded KGB cables from the period.

2. *VENONA: Decoding Soviet Espionage in America*, John Earl Haynes and Harvey Klehr. Yale University Press, 1999. Excellent analysis of declassified VENONA transcripts that includes a cogent assessment of the insight they provide about J. Robert Oppenheimer.

3. *Wedge: From Pearl Harbor to 9/11, How the Secret War between the FBI and the CIA Has Endangered National Security*, Mark Riebling. Simon and Schuster, 1994. Predating the declassification of VENONA, this is, nonetheless, an excellent general history of American counterintelligence, notwithstanding the melodramatic title.

4. *Spycraft: A Secret History of the CIA's Spytechs from Communism to Al-Qaeda*, Robert Wallace and Keith Melton. Penguin Books, 2008. This excellent history of spy technology includes an explanation of one-time pads, as well as a real-life practice exercise on how to use them. It also includes the KGB photos of the arrest of Adolf Tolkachev.

9 The Last Act Begins
Santa Fe, September 21, 1985

WHERE: The western side of the Y intersection of Garcia Street and Camino Corrales.

WHAT: At this spot, former CIA officer Edward Lee Howard leapt out from the passenger side of the moving car driven by his wife, Mary, into the bushes along the road. Once certain that he had successfully evaded FBI surveillance, Howard escaped and defected to Moscow, where he revealed the two most important operations that the CIA ever ran in the Soviet Union. Code-named GTTAW and GTVANQUISH, they were instrumental to America's prevailing in the Cold War against the Soviet Union. In 2002, a drunken, and by-then divorced, Howard reportedly fell down a flight of stairs in Moscow and died, unmourned, of a broken neck.[1]

During his first term in office, President Ronald Reagan fundamentally changed America's strategy toward the Soviet Union. Since the nuclear fright of the Cuban Missile Crisis, American policy had been to encourage stable relations with the Soviets. This emphasis on stability had led American strategic thinkers to the nuclear-arms concept of mutually assured destruction (MAD). MAD proponents insisted on the counterintuitive argument that the best defense against nuclear attack was for America and the Soviet Union to leave themselves defenseless. If both countries were mutually assured of total destruction in a nuclear war, then neither country would start one.

The need for strategic stability and the MAD concept were used by American strategists in the 1960s and early 1970s as justification for allowing the Soviets to reach nuclear parity with America. Unfortunately, the Soviets saw no need to slow down their strategic-weapons programs once they reached parity. Quite the contrary. Soviet strategic thinkers were aiming for Soviet dominance, not for mutually assured destruction.

President Reagan clearly saw Soviet behavior for what it was. Stability on Soviet terms was unacceptable to him. He saw that Soviet communism had lost its ideological appeal even to officers of the KGB, who were sworn to serve as "the Sword and the Shield of the Soviet Communist Party." He understood that Moscow's heavy investments in strategic-weapons programs were driving the Soviet economy to the breaking point. So President Reagan decided to drive the Soviets over the edge.

On March 23, 1983, President Reagan repudiated MAD and announced the Strategic Defense Initiative (SDI), also known as Star Wars. Reagan made the common-sense argument that the best way to eliminate the risk of nuclear was to render nuclear weapons "impotent and obsolete." Reagan asked, "What if we could intercept and destroy strategic ballistic missiles before they reached our own soil or that of our allies?"[2]

In announcing SDI, Reagan knew that he was opening a new arena of strategic competition between America and the Soviet Union in which the Soviets could not compete. The Soviet economy was already taxed to the breaking point. Moreover, SDI exploited America's widening lead in advanced technology, particularly advanced computer technology.

President Reagan's strategic gamble was based on the best intelligence America ever had on the Soviet Union. American listening posts ringed the Soviet Union, recording every internal communication they could. American spy satellites photographed all Soviet military activity. The CIA and FBI had recruited a dozen or more disillusioned KGB officers to serve as American spies deep inside the corrupt Soviet security agency. Most important of all, the CIA had GTVANQUISH and GTTAW.

GTVANQUISH was the code name for Adolf Tolkachev, a top Russian weapons engineer. Tolkachev was arguably the most important clandestine agent the CIA has ever had. Between 1979 and 1985, Tolkachev provided volumes of technical information that revealed the vulnerabilities of Russian advanced weapons systems. This information would have assured dominant American air superiority in case of war with the Soviet Union.

Despite the mortal danger, Tolkachev declined to use classic clandestine tradecraft methods like dead drops, preferring face-to-face personal meetings. He insisted on meetings because they enabled him to pass the maximum amount of information in the shortest period of time. In so doing, Tolkachev hoped to (and did) hasten the demise of the corrupt Soviet regime, which he despised.

GTTAW was the code name for a real-life "mission impossible." A top-secret, underground, communications cable connected the Soviet nuclear-weapons research-and-development complex with the Soviet Ministry of Defense. The KGB was confident that America's CIA did not know that this cable existed. The KGB was very confident that, even if the CIA learned that the cable existed, it could never figure out exactly where it was located. The KGB was *supremely* confident that even if the CIA figured out exactly where the cable was located, CIA officers working in Moscow under pervasive KGB surveillance would never be able to get physically close to the cable. The Soviets were so confident in the KGB's ability to protect this top-secret underground cable that they did not bother to encrypt the top-secret communications that traveled along it between the Soviet Ministry of Defense and the Soviet nuclear-weapons complex!

Hubris is always unwise. Hubris in the high-stakes world of modern espionage is particularly unwise. Nonetheless, hubris is relatively commonplace among highly successful intelligence officers, no matter what their nationality. It qualifies as something of an occupational hazard for intelligence officers.

In this case, the Soviet KGB paid dearly for their hubris. The CIA did learn of the top-secret underground communications cable. It did learn exactly where it was located. And despite the KGB's vaunted surveillance capabilities, CIA officers serving in Moscow did get physical access to that top-secret cable . . . with great regularity.

Once a month or so for six years—dozens and dozens of times—a CIA officer would take a walk in Moscow, accompanied by 20–25 KGB surveillants. At some point during the walk, the CIA officer would lose the KGB surveillance team, without the team realizing that they had lost the CIA officer. Once certain that he or she had evaded the surveillance, the CIA officer would proceed to the destination, remove a manhole cover, climb down the manhole, remove a recording tape from the Soviet unencrypted, top-secret, underground communications cable, and replace it with a new recording tape. Then the officer would climb back out of the manhole, replace the manhole cover, and take the recording tape back to his or her office.[3]

Just imagine! *Every* communication between the Soviet nuclear-weapons complex and the Soviet Ministry of Defense for six years!

Then, suddenly, the CIA's well of top-secret Soviet information dried up. In March 1985, a CIA officer made the regular run to pick up the GTTAW tapes. When she went down the manhole, she discovered to her chagrin that all the recording equipment was gone. The Soviets had evidently discovered the operation. The CIA officer fully expected to be arrested by a team of unhappy KGB officers when she climbed back out of the manhole.

She was not arrested, however. The KGB just let her go. They were so embarrassed that the CIA had been able to pull off this operation right under their noses that they didn't want to draw attention to it. The KGB wanted GTTAW to go away quietly.

The KGB was less kind to GTVANQUISH, weapons engineer Adolf Tolkachev, the greatest spy in CIA history. In April 1985, just weeks after GTTAW ended, the KGB arrested Tolkachev, interrogated him roughly, and then executed him with a pistol bullet to the temple. Tolkachev never got to witness the demise of the Soviet regime that he helped bring about.

Then, in August that same year, the CIA learned from a KGB defector that GTTAW and GTVANQUISH had been betrayed by a wretched, midlevel employee of the New Mexico state government named Edward Lee Howard.

Before moving to Santa Fe, Howard had been a CIA clandestine-operations officer. Indeed, he was a member of the elite group of CIA officers selected to serve their very first tour in Moscow supporting the GTTAW and GTVANQUISH operations. He was one of the CIA officers specially trained to beat the 20–25 person KGB surveillance teams on the streets of Moscow. After the training, Howard became cocky and began to use his new clandestine skills to commit petty larceny, just because he knew he could get away with it.

When Howard's superior at the CIA, Burton Gerber, learned of his behavior during a routine lie-detector test, Howard was abruptly fired. He never got to work in Moscow, but he did know about GTTAW and GTVANQUISH. To get revenge, Howard made clandestine contact with the KGB in late 1984 and told them all about the CIA's two most important operations.

The counterintelligence office at CIA knew something was amiss after GTTAW disappeared and GTVANQUISH was arrested. Counterintelligence learned exactly what had happened in August 1985, when KGB Colonel Vitali Yurchenko defected in Rome. Yurchenko told the CIA about a young Moscow-bound CIA officer who had been fired as a result of his personal behavior. Yurchenko did not know the officer's name but said that his KGB code name was ROBERT. According to Yurchenko, it was ROBERT who had told the KGB about GTTAW and GTVANQUISH.

Counterintelligence at CIA recognized immediately that ROBERT was Edward Lee Howard and so advised the FBI. In turn, the FBI office in New Mexico put Howard under intense surveillance, the same kind that Howard had been trained to identify and to beat.

Recognizing that he was about to be arrested, and panicked by the thought of serving prison time, Howard decided to defect to the Soviet Union. To make good his escape from the country, Howard needed 12 to 18 hours of lead time before the FBI surveillance team would realize that he was gone. For this, Howard needed his wife, Mary, to aid and abet his escape. He also needed to convince Mary that the FBI would not be upset with her for helping him escape; everything would be OK. She and their son could rejoin Howard later.[4]

Howard and his family were living in a house at 108 Verano Loop, in the bedroom community of Eldorado, south of Santa Fe. He arranged for a babysitter on the evening of Saturday, September 21, so that he and Mary could go out for dinner at a restaurant on Canyon Road named Alphonso's; today it is the well-known restaurant Geronimo's. Howard intentionally tried to alert the FBI of their dinner plans, because, to gain the needed lead time, he had to lull the FBI into thinking that nothing was amiss.

Due to the blinding New Mexico sunset, the FBI agents parked nearby did not see Howard and Mary depart their house. Howard not only expected the agents to follow them, he *wanted* the agents to follow them. CIA officers are comfortable operating under surveillance as long as they can see and manipulate it. What makes them nervous is not being able to see surveillance that they know is there. Howard knew he was under FBI surveillance, but the surveillance teams did not follow them. Why?

Howard and Mary ran a well-prepared "surveillance-detection route" on their way to the restaurant. They proceeded along Old Pecos Trail into central Santa Fe. Just before the State Capitol Building, they turned right onto Paseo de Peralta. Then, just fifty meters short of the Paseo de Peralta Bridge (where Klaus Fuchs and Harry Gold had met in 1945), Howard and Mary turned onto Canyon Road, which runs one way, west to east. Howard had planned these two natural and nonalerting turns to enable him to identify the FBI surveillance cars that he knew had to be behind him. But he still could not see the FBI surveillance. Why?

At the restaurant, Howard decided to telephone the babysitter to let her know where they were and how long they intended to be there. Of course, they had already told the babysitter that information; his real intent was to reassure the FBI one more time that nothing was amiss; Howard was not about to escape to Moscow. He and Mary were just out for a Saturday night dinner together. Unfortunately, the FBI agent responsible for monitoring Howard's telephone was taking a short break and missed the call.

After dinner, Howard got in the front passenger seat and let Mary drive. The FBI knew he was an alcoholic, so this would seem natural to any watching FBI surveillant. Mary turned right out of the restaurant's parking lot onto Camino del Monte Sol. Their natural route home would take them directly south, back to Old Santa Fe Trail; Howard expected FBI surveillance both behind them and in front of them.

At the first stop sign, rather than continuing straight along Camino del Monte Sol, Mary performed a "reverse," turning almost 180 degrees onto the narrow, one-way street Acequia Madre. This was an aggressive countersurveillance maneuver designed to lose any surveillants in front of the Howards and to force those behind to reveal themselves. Still, Howard did not see the FBI surveillance cars that he *knew* must be there!

Now Howard was really starting to worry. They were on the final leg of his well-prepared surveillance-detection route to the spot where he planned to leap out of the car. Yet he still could not see the surveillance. Why?

Mary drove to the western end of Acequia Madre Street and turned left onto Garcia Street, which rises gently up a hill, past the School of American Research, to a Y intersection with Camino Corrales. As a car follows the bend around the gentle curve onto Camino Corrales, for a brief moment it is out of sight of any car following it, even one following closely.

At that exact moment, Howard leapt out of the car and hid in the bushes along the road. Simultaneously, Mary popped up a silhouette dummy in the passenger seat to make it appear to anybody behind her that there were still two people in the car. She then turned south onto Old Santa Fe Trail and resumed her drive home. The first time that the FBI agents realized that the Howards had even left the house was when they saw Mary drive back into the garage. They weren't worried, however, because they saw two silhouettes in the car. The Howards were back home for the night, or so the FBI thought.

In fact, once certain that he had successfully evaded any FBI surveillance, Howard walked from Camino Corrales north along Old Santa Fe Trail to the Inn at Loretto, where he boarded a shuttle bus to the Albuquerque airport. He paid cash for a ticket to Tucson, Arizona. The next morning, Sunday, September 22, Howard flew from Tucson to Helsinki and then, with KGB assistance, escaped to Moscow on September 24.

Both the FBI and the CIA were deeply embarrassed by Howard's successful escape. A young FBI special agent was reprimanded for failing to notice Howard and Mary leaving the house and for missing the telephone call from the restaurant. The CIA, for its part, was severely criticized for failing to warn the FBI that Howard was an expert in countersurveillance techniques. Moreover, shortly after Howard escaped, Vitali Yurchenko, the KGB defector who had first alerted the CIA to ROBERT, redefected back to the Soviet Union and resumed working for the KGB, making the CIA look foolish and leading many to believe that Yurchenko's supposed defection was fake from the very start.

Mary Howard bore her share of the FBI's anger about the case but was never prosecuted for aiding and abetting Howard's escape. Nobody wanted another controversy similar to that related to Ethel Rosenberg. Mary eventually divorced Howard.

Howard descended deeper and deeper into alcoholism, becoming a significant nuisance for his KGB hosts. In 2002, a drunken Howard fell—some say he was pushed—down a flight of stairs and broke his neck. The KGB cremated his body, however, before the family arrived in Moscow to confirm his death.

The comprehensive intelligence regarding Soviet weapons systems produced by GTVANQUISH and GTTAW enhanced the possibility that President Reagan's Strategic Defense Initiative would actually work. However, the technical feasibility of Star Wars almost didn't matter. When they learned about GTVANQUISH and GTTAW, the stunned Soviet leadership had to assume that SDI would work very well, indeed.

The new Soviet leader, Mikhail Gorbachev, knew that he had no strategic choice except to negotiate real nuclear-arms reductions with President Reagan. President Reagan knew it, as well. Most importantly, both Gorbachev and Reagan knew that the other knew . . .

Suggestions for Further Reading

1. "Tolkachev: A Worthy Successor to Penkovsky, An Exceptional Espionage Operation," Barry Royden. *Studies in Intelligence*, Vol. 47, Number 3, 2003. A declassified study of one of CIA's greatest operations. Now available to the public on the CIA Web site.

2. *The Cold War: A New History*, John Lewis Gaddis. Penguin Books, 2005. The essential primer on the history of the Cold War.

3. *The Spy Who Got Away: The Inside Story of Edward Lee Howard, the CIA Agent Who Betrayed His Country's Secrets and Escaped to Moscow*, David Wise. Random House, 1998. A professional and balanced account of the Howard case.

4. *Safe House: The Compelling Memoirs of the Only CIA Spy to Seek Asylum in Russia*, Edward Lee Howard. Enigma Books, 1995. Howard's side of the story, for what it's worth. A terrible, self-serving book by a despicable human being.

10 Here We Go Again?
Santa Fe, 1999

WHERE: 80 Barcelona Avenue, White Rock, New Mexico, twenty miles northwest of Santa Fe.

WHAT: This modest house is where Dr. Wen Ho Lee lived in the late 1990s, when he was suspected of nuclear espionage on behalf of the People's Republic of China. The Wen Ho Lee case became as politically controversial in its time as the Rosenberg and Oppenheimer cases were in the early 1950s. It took more than forty years before historians were given sufficient access to declassified information from the VENONA project to enable them to reach definitive judgments regarding the Rosenbergs and Ted Hall, on one hand, and J. Robert Oppenheimer on the other. In 2000, Dr. Lee pleaded guilty to one felony charge of unauthorized possession and control of restricted data relating to U.S. national defense in exchange for the U.S. government's dropping fifty-eight more serious charges. This plea bargain kept the government from having to provide public access to classified information in an open courtroom. In 2006, Dr. Lee received a $1.6 million settlement for violations of his privacy rights and reportedly retired in Albuquerque.

Wen Ho Lee was born in Taiwan in 1939. He immigrated to the United States in 1965 and earned a PhD in mechanical engineering from Texas A&M University in 1969. He became a naturalized U.S. citizen in 1974 and began work at Los Alamos National Laboratories in 1978.[1]

Dr. Lee first came to the attention of the FBI on December 3, 1982, when he telephoned a Taiwan-born scientist living in California named Min Guobao. Dr. Min had been forced to resign his job at Lawrence Livermore National Laboratory in 1981 after coming under suspicion of espionage and of mishandling nuclear-weaons-related information. FBI wiretaps of Min's phone recorded the call from Dr. Lee, during which Lee reportedly offered to find out who had betrayed Min, an offer that Min declined. On November 9, 1983, the FBI questioned Lee about his relationship with Min. Lee denied knowing Min or calling Min until he was confronted with the taped telephone conversation. Subsequently, Dr. Lee agreed to and passed an FBI polygraph related to his relationship with Dr. Min.[2]

As a result of the Min Guobao incident, the director of security at Los Alamos recommended, as a prudent risk-management measure, to transfer Dr. Lee from nuclear-weapons work to less sensitive work. Had this recommendation been accepted, history would have turned out differently, and arguably better, from every perspective: that of U.S. national security, of Los Alamos National Laboratory, and of Dr. Wen Ho Lee. Unfortunately, the recommendation was rejected by the lab director for unknown reasons.[3]

Dr. Lee again came to FBI attention twelve years later, in February 1994, when the head of the Chinese nuclear-weapons program, Hu Side, gave Lee a warm, personal greeting during an official meeting at Los Alamos. Dr. Hu had been the lead designer of a miniaturized nuclear weapon the Chinese had tested in 1992, a weapon that purportedly appeared remarkably similar to America's most advanced nuclear warhead, the W-88. It was suspicious that Dr. Lee knew somebody of Hu's high rank in the Chinese nuclear-weapons program and even more suspicious that Dr. Lee had never reported this important relationship as he was required to do. On the other hand, it made no sense that Hu would publicly greet Lee if Lee had a clandestine relationship with the Chinese government.[4]

Five years later, the U.S. government learned how Wen Ho Lee had come to know Hu Side. In December 1998, Dr. Lee admitted to Department of Energy counterintelligence officials that ten years earlier, during a visit to Beijing, he had been visited in his hotel room by two Chinese scientists. Lee admitted that they asked him questions about classified details of miniaturized nuclear weapons like the W-88. Lee asserted that he refused to discuss the matter with the Chinese scientists and that he didn't know the answer to their questions in any case. Asked why he had failed to report this important contact, Dr. Lee told the counterintelligence officials that he had simply forgotten to do so. Then, in a subsequent interview with the FBI, Dr. Lee admitted that one of the two scientists who had come to his hotel room was Hu Side.[5]

The facts are most certainly suspicious. They might constitute grounds for revoking a person's security clearance, but they are not sufficient to prove that somebody has committed espionage. To prove espionage, the U.S. government must have evidence that a person has passed classified information to a foreign power with the intent to injure the United States. In this case, there would have been no such evidence unless (1) Dr. Lee himself confessed or (2) Hu Side or somebody else from the Chinese government agreed to provide testimony in a U.S. court of law.

Department of Energy counterintelligence asked Dr. Lee if he would be willing to take a polygraph exam. The specific focus of the exam would be whether Dr. Lee had ever given classified information to representatives of the Chinese government, including the two Chinese scientists who had visited him in his Beijing hotel room in 1988. Dr. Lee readily consented to take the polygraph exam.

This polygraph was conducted on December 23, 1998, by an experienced polygrapher who worked for the Department of Energy counterintelligence program. Dr. Lee denied ever having given classified information to the Chinese. His denial was assessed as being "not deceptive." In other words, the assessment was that Dr. Lee had passed the lie detector test.

When other experienced polygraphers working for the FBI reviewed the same results one month later, they reached the opposite conclusion. Ultimately, the FBI assessed Dr. Lee's polygraph results as "inconclusive" at best and probably "deceptive." Therefore, the FBI asked Dr. Lee whether he would be willing to take another polygraph exam. Again, Dr. Lee readily consented to do so.

This polygraph was conducted by the FBI on February 10, 1999. Again, Dr. Lee denied ever having given classified information to any unauthorized person, including the Chinese. This time, his denial was assessed as being "deceptive." The FBI polygrapher told Dr. Lee that he had failed this second lie-detector test. During a postpolygraph interview, Dr. Lee admitted that in 1986 a Chinese nuclear-weapons specialist named Wei Shenli had asked him for assistance with a math equation used in classified nuclear-weapons work. Dr. Lee admitted that he had provided the requested assistance but, again, denied that he had revealed any classified information.[6]

These conflicting polygraph results did little to clarify the facts of the situation. None of them was legally admissible in court. They did result, however, in years of controversy among the scientists working within America's national laboratories about the scientific reliability of polygraph exams.

On Saturday, March 6, 1999, the *New York Times* ran a front-page article, based on leaks of classified information from government officials, about a Chinese American scientist at Los Alamos who was suspected of providing nuclear-weapons secrets to the People's Republic of China. Dr. Lee was not identified by name, but it was clear to his family and friends that he was the suspect. The article compared this case to the Rosenberg case of the 1950s in terms of damage to U.S. national security. That same afternoon, an FBI agent called Dr. Lee and arranged to meet with him the next day.

That Sunday, two FBI agents conducted an unusually confrontational interview with Dr. Lee. Generally, interviews by FBI counterintelligence officers are designed to avoid confrontation because patient, low-key approaches are judged more productive in winning cooperation. In this case, however, it appears that the heightened publicity was causing urgency for the FBI to get to the bottom of what had happened in that Beijing hotel room in 1988. The confrontational interview did not go well for either Dr. Lee or the FBI.[7]

On the very next day, March 8, 1999, Dr. Lee was fired from Los Alamos on grounds that he had failed to properly notify Energy Department and lab officials about contacts with people from a sensitive country. Dr. Lee had admitted that on two occasions he had been asked for classified information from Chinese nuclear-weapons specialists: by Wen Shenli in 1986 and by Hu Side in 1988. Although Dr. Lee had denied that he had ever provided classified information to Wei, Hu, or any other unauthorized person, he admitted that he had not reported the highly suspicious requests until a decade later.

The FBI searched both his office and his home. Computer forensics established that Dr. Lee had transferred a large amount of data from the classified computer network at Los Alamos to an unclassified computer at the lab, in violation of Energy Department and lab security regulations. The transfer of the data took nearly forty hours over seventy days in 1993–1994. Much of the data was unrelated to Dr. Lee's own work and responsibilities. Dr. Lee then downloaded the information onto ten portable computer tapes.

Dr. Lee initially denied having downloaded the information onto the computer tapes but, when confronted with the forensic evidence, admitted that he had done so. Three of the tapes were discovered in Dr. Lee's office. The other seven were nowhere to be found. Dr. Lee initially indicated that he had destroyed them. Subsequently, he said that he had thrown them into a trash bin at the lab. The ultimate disposition of the seven missing tapes was never determined.[8]

At this point, the U.S. government had ample evidence to charge Dr. Lee with a felony count of illegally gathering and retaining national-security information. However, the government either (1) did not have sufficient evidence to prove that Dr. Lee had, with the intent to injure the United States, given those tapes to some foreign country—an act of espionage—or (2) was not prepared to reveal publicly in a court of law the information that it did have, as had happened in the case of Ted Hall (see chapter 8).

It was at the indictment-and-detention stage that the Wen Ho Lee case *really* went awry. On December 10, 1999, Dr. Lee was indicted on fifty-nine felony counts. Twenty counts were for unlawfully gathering and retaining national-security information, each count carrying a maximum sentence of ten years in prison. The additional thirty-nine counts were for receiving nuclear-weapons-related restricted data with intent to injure the United States or with intent to secure an advantage to any foreign nation, each count carrying a maximum sentence of life in prison.

Dr. Lee was denied bail on the grounds that he posed a clear-and-present danger to the security of the United States. He was held in solitary confinement at the Santa Fe County Detention Center for nine months, from December 10, 1999, until September 13, 2000. A light burned constantly in his room. He was released only one hour a day for exercise and could see his family only one hour a week. When he did leave solitary confinement, Dr. Lee was handcuffed and shackled.[9]

Such harsh treatment of a respected community member like Dr. Lee was highly unusual, especially given the limited information publicly available. What motivated the government to impose such harsh treatment? Did partisan politics in Washington, D.C., play a role? Did U.S.-China tensions exert an influence? Was there racial prejudice? Did the government hope to intimidate Dr. Lee into greater cooperation regarding the seven missing tapes? Was it some uncoordinated blend of all of these factors? I do not know the answers to those questions.

I do know that whatever the motivation, the harsh treatment proved to be completely counterproductive. In the court of American public opinion, it was judged totally disproportionate to the publicly offered evidence of wrongdoing. Americans of all ethnic and political backgrounds were embarrassed and disappointed.

In September 2000, fifty-eight of the fifty-nine charges against Dr. Lee were dropped. In exchange, Dr. Lee pleaded guilty to one felony count of illegally gathering and retaining national-security information and was sentenced to the ten months in jail, already served. At the same time, Dr. Lee received an extraordinary public apology from the federal judge who presided at his trial. According to newspapers at the time, Judge James Parker stated in court, "I believe you were terribly wronged by being held in custody pretrial in the Santa Fe County Detention Center under demeaning, unnecessarily punitive, conditions. I am truly sorry."

In 2006, Dr. Lee received a $1.6 million settlement for violations of his rights under the Privacy Act. As of 2009, he and his wife, Sylvia, were reportedly retired and living quietly in Albuquerque.[10]

In discussions of the Wen Ho Lee case, people frequently ask whether I believe Chinese Americans are more susceptible than other Americans to recruitment by Chinese intelligence. My response is that Chinese Americans are no more susceptible to recruitment in general than any other American ethnic group. However, if a specific individual Chinese American is susceptible to recruitment in general, then that Chinese American would probably be more susceptible to recruitment by Chinese intelligence than, say, by Russian intelligence. The same would be true for Russian

Americans or Iranian Americans or Irish Americans. The same would be equally true for me; in general, I would not be a good recruitment target for any foreign intelligence service, but Chinese intelligence would probably have a better chance targeting me than Russian or Irish intelligence, simply because I have greater knowledge of and affinity for Chinese culture than I do Russian or Irish culture.

People also frequently ask me whether naturalization as an American citizen provides any measure of protection against recruitment by the intelligence service of the person's birth country. In fact, first-generation Americans, as a group, will demonstrate *both* a higher degree of American patriotism and a higher degree of susceptibility to recruitment by their birth country's intelligence service; it all depends on the individual's motivation for becoming a naturalized American citizen. If naturalization is simply a matter of economic convenience for the person, then cultural affinity may make that person somewhat more willing to cooperate with his birth country's intelligence service. On the other hand, a first-generation immigrant who wants to become part of the American Dream will generally be more patriotic than many people whose families have lived here for generations.

A friend of mine who is a first-generation immigrant from the former Soviet Union recently named his newborn daughter "America." As a professional intelligence officer, I can say with some confidence that fellow will never present a risk to U.S. national security.

Suggestions for Further Reading

1. *The Anatomy of an Investigation: The Difficult Case(s) of Wen Ho Lee*, Kirsten Lundberg, with sponsors Philip Heymann and Jessica Stern. Harvard Kennedy School of Government Case Study Program, 2001. A very balanced treatment of this most controversial case.

2. *My Country Versus Me: The First-Hand Account of the Los Alamos Scientist Who Was Falsely Accused of Being a Spy*, Wen Ho Lee, with Helen Zia. Hyperion Press, 2001. Wen Ho Lee provides his perspective on his ordeal. A partial transcript of his confrontational interview with the FBI is included on pages 75–83.

3. *Code Name Kindred Spirit: Inside the Chinese Nuclear Espionage Scandal*, Notra Trulock. Encounter Books, 2003. Notra Trulock's response to Wen Ho Lee's book. History would have turned out better for everyone, perhaps, had the 1984 recommendation, noted on page 76, to transfer Dr. Lee to less-sensitive work been accepted.

4. *A Convenient Spy: Wen Ho Lee and the Politics of Nuclear Espionage*, Dan Stober and Ian Hoffman. Simon and Schuster, 2001. This is another solid account of the Wen Ho Lee affair by two well-informed journalists.

Conclusion
Past as Prologue

KEY POINT: New Mexico is as much of interest to foreign-intelligence officers today as it was in the 1940s. The reason is quite simple: Cutting-edge scientific and technical information, like that produced at Los Alamos and Sandia National Laboratories, has great value. As long as such information (sometimes known as intellectual property) has value, powerful nations will employ intelligence officers to steal it. They also will employ *counterintelligence* officers to keep potential adversary nations from stealing the valuable information they wish to protect. This is a fact of life about which we need not be paranoid . . . but of which all Americans should be aware.

In retrospect, it is clear that two wise counterintelligence decisions made by General Leslie Groves in 1942 still profoundly affect daily life in New Mexico today, although few New Mexicans realize it. Groves's first counterintelligence decision made common sense: to locate America's new atomic-weapons-design laboratory in the "middle of nowhere" in order to make it as difficult as possible for foreign-intelligence officers to communicate with spies they might have working inside that laboratory. Groves's second counterintelligence decision was a bit riskier: to approve a top-secret security clearance for J. Robert Oppenheimer despite his known history of flirtation with communists. Without that security clearance, Oppenheimer, like Albert Einstein, would have been excluded from deep involvement in the Manhattan Project.

Because he *was* selected to be the lab director, Oppenheimer got to select the "middle of nowhere" that would become the site for the atomic-weapons-design laboratory. As we saw in chapter 3, he chose a place he loved: Los Alamos. In 1949, the engineering division of Los Alamos, then called the Z Division, was moved to Albuquerque and renamed Sandia National Laboratories. Over time, Sandia has grown in size to match its parent laboratory, Los Alamos.

Today, Los Alamos and Sandia are two of the premier scientific and technological institutions in the world. They are also two of the largest employers in New Mexico, providing over fifteen thousand well-paying jobs directly and tens of thousands more jobs indirectly, in arenas including high-tech support firms, schools, restaurants, construction companies, department stores, and hospitals. The labs were also among the first big customers for a small company founded in Albuquerque in 1975 by a Harvard dropout. The dropout's name was Bill Gates and the company was named Microsoft. The labs also invented "clean rooms," which are foundational elements of today's microelectronics industry.

The mission of Los Alamos and Sandia—the reason the two labs exist—is U.S. national security. Originally, that mission translated narrowly into a scientific and technological focus on nuclear weapons. Over time, the technical focus of the labs has expanded far beyond nuclear weapons. But the mission focus remains the same as it has always been—U.S. national security.

That continuing mission focus on national security means that Los Alamos and Sandia continue to merit the attention of foreign-intelligence officers. This is quite natural; it is what intelligence officers do for a living. However, today New Mexico is no longer in the middle of nowhere, and nothing prevents foreign-intelligence officers from traveling to New Mexico from New York City. Even more significant, nothing prevents foreign-intelligence officers from communicating with people inside these national-security laboratories via cell phone, e-mail, or social networking sites. From a strictly logistical standpoint then, it is easier than ever for an intelligence officer to communicate with a spy. So what is a counterintelligence officer to do?

Today, successful counterintelligence in New Mexico, as elsewhere, depends, first and foremost, on the support and cooperation from the community of people who create the valuable information and intellectual property in the first place. To be truly successful, modern counterintelligence must foster healthy communities that are not paranoid . . . but are alert to the real threat posed by foreign-intelligence services and are motivated by prudent self-interest to counter that threat. If 999 out of every 1,000 people in the community are aware that foreign-intelligence officers really are trying to spot and assess the 1 person out of 1,000 who might be tempted to betray secrets, the chances of detecting and defeating the efforts of those foreign-intelligence officers early become much higher. Adversary intelligence services will fail when (1) the community has sufficient trust in counterintelligence to report indications that someone (like Ted Hall) intends to spy and (2) people with valuable information (like J. Robert Oppenheimer) choose, on their own accord, not to spy.

Notes

Introduction

1. Christopher Andrew and Vasili Mitokhin, *The Sword and the Shield: The Mitrokhin Archive and the Secret History of the KGB* (New York: Basic Books, 1999), 107.

Chapter One

1. Pavel Sudoplatov and Anatoli Sudoplatov, *Special Tasks: The Memoirs of an Unwanted Witness—A Soviet Spymaster*, with Jerrold L. and Leona P. Schecter (New York: Little, Brown and Company, 1994). The security and intelligence service of the Soviet Union was known by many names during its seventy-year history. This book uses only the name most familiar to Americans, the KGB.

Chapter Two

1. Pavel Sudoplatov and Anatoli Sudoplatov, *Special Tasks*, 63–86.
2. For prewar Nazi disinformation efforts against Stalin, see Edward Jay Epstein, *Deception: The Invisible War Between the KGB and the CIA* (New York: Simon and Shuster, 1989). For a chilling historical account of the Wannsee Conference, see the brilliant HBO film *Conspiracy: One Meeting, Six Million Lives*, starring Kenneth Branagh as Reinhard Heydrich and Stanley Tucci as Heydrich's aide, Adolf Eichmann.
3. See Thomas C. Reed, *At the Abyss: An Insider's History of the Cold War* (New York: Random House, 2004), 24–26; and Amy Knight, *Beria: Stalin's First Lieutenant* (Princeton, NJ: Princeton University Press, 1993), 176–80. Beria canceled Stalin's order for Grigulevich

to assassinate Tito in 1953 after, as some believe, Beria had Stalin assassinated.

4. Ronald Radosh, "Even Worse Than We Thought," *Los Angeles Times Sunday Book Review*, June 30, 2002.

5. "Obituary, Katie Zook," *Albuquerque Journal*, May 12, 1998.

Chapter Three

1. Allen Weinstein and Alexander Vassiliev, *The Haunted Wood: Soviet Espionage in America—The Stalin Era* (New York: Random House, 1999), 208. This deals with the Friday, May 11, 1945, meeting of Sax and Yatskov in New York City. Since Sunday was the only day that Hall could leave Los Alamos, his meeting with Sax in Albuquerque almost certainly took place the previous Sunday, May 6.

2. Ibid., 172–222.

3. Albert Einstein played an instrumental role in convincing President Franklin Roosevelt to commit America to building an atomic weapon during World War II. Nonetheless, Manhattan Project leaders did not consider Einstein sufficiently trustworthy to be given direct access to the top-secret details of the actual work.

4. Gregg Herken, *Brotherhood of the Bomb* (New York: Henry Holt and Company, 2002), 83-121.

5. Ibid., 129. Alternatively, Los Alamos historian Marjorie Bell Chambers believes that the reference to Trinity has Hindu roots rather than Christian. See Ferenc Szasz, *Larger Than Life: New Mexico in the Twentieth Century* (Albuquerque: University of New Mexico Press, 2006), 40.

6. Oleg Nechiporenko, *Passport to Assassination: The Never-Before-Told Story of Lee Harvey Oswald by the KGB Colonel Who Knew Him* (Secaucus, NJ: Carol Publishing, 1993).

7. Aleksandr Feklisov, *The Man Behind the Rosenbergs* (New York: Enigma Books, 2004), 295-359.

8. Allen Weinstein and Alexander Vassiliev, *The Haunted Wood*, 172-222.

9. Joseph Albright and Marcia Kunstel, *Bombshell* (New York: Random House, 1997), 91-99.

10. Ibid., 110-11. However, see note 1 above for the May 6 meeting in Albuquerque.

11. Ibid., 114. We know from this that the meeting took place in the vicinity of the train station in downtown Albuquerque. We also know from Hall that Saville Sax was notoriously forgetful. So it is highly likely that Hall would have chosen an easy-to-remember venue like First and Central for their predesignated meeting spot.

12. Allen Weinstein and Alexander Vassiliev, *The Haunted Wood*, 208.

13. A gun-type atomic bomb is quite simple: One subcritical mass of highly enriched weapons-grade uranium-235 is "shot" at high

speed into another subcritical mass of U-235. The two subcritical masses add up to one critical mass, causing a chain reaction that results in an atomic explosion. Although simple in design, a gun-type bomb requires a large mass of weapons-grade U-235, which is difficult and expensive to produce. Plutonium was easier to produce than U-235 during the Manhattan Project era. Moreover, a smaller amount of plutonium is required to reach a critical mass. Plutonium cannot be used in a simple gun-type design, however, because it detonates before initiation of an atomic powered chain reaction. To use plutonium to produce an atomic-force explosion, Los Alamos scientists had to develop an implosion-type atomic bomb. In that type of bomb, a sphere of plutonium is surrounded by a number of intricate explosive lenses that drive the explosive force inward, i.e., an implosion. This implosion compresses the plutonium into a critical mass. Then an initiator triggers the atomic chain reaction.

14. Allen Weinstein and Alexander Vassiliev, *The Haunted Wood*, 208.
15. Ibid., 209.
16. Robert Louis Benson and Michael Warner, eds., VENONA: *Soviet Espionage and the American Response, 1939–1957* (Washington, D.C.: National Security Agency and the Central Intelligence Agency, 1996), 441–42; and Joseph Albright and Marcia Kunstel, *Bombshell*, 143–47.

Chapter Four

1. Robert Chadwell Williams, *Klaus Fuchs: Atom Spy* (Boston: Harvard University Press, 1987); and, Allen Weinstein and Alexander Vassiliev, *The Haunted Wood*, 210. The confession of Harry Gold to the FBI.
2. Soviet Military Intelligence—the GRU—met with Fuchs in England. When Fuchs transferred to America, the KGB took over responsibility for meeting him. Fuchs himself neither knew nor cared which Soviet intelligence service he met.
3. Allen Weinstein and Alexander Vassiliev, *The Haunted Wood*, 203.
4. Ibid., 209.
5. Ibid., 204.
6. Robert Chadwell Williams, *Klaus Fuchs: Atom Spy*.
7. Joseph Albright and Marcia Kunstel, *Bombshell*, 140–41.
8. Richard Rhodes, *Dark Sun: The Making of the Hydrogen Bomb* (New York: Simon and Schuster, 1995), 175–76.
9. John Dower, *Embracing Defeat: Japan in the Wake of World War II* (New York: W.W. Norton and Company, 1999), 51–52.

Chapter Five

1. Richard Melzer, *Breakdown: How the Secret of the Atomic Bomb Was Stolen during World War II* (Santa Fe: Sunstone Press, 2000), 102-4.
2. Richard Rhodes, *Dark Sun*, 138.
3. Allen Weinstein and Alexander Vassiliev, *The Haunted Wood*, 198.
4. Richard Rhodes, *Dark Sun*, 139.
5. Aleksandr Feklisov, *The Man Behind the Rosenbergs*, 246.

Chapter Six

1. Joseph Albright and Marcia Kunstel, *Bombshell*, 148-58.
2. Ibid., 149-50; Allen Weinstein and Alexander Vassiliev, *The Haunted Wood*, 211. Ted Hall's comments indicate that this meeting on the UNM campus with Lona Cohen took place after the July 16 Trinity test. Lona Cohen met with Anatoli Yatskov in New York City in mid-August to pass along the information she had received from Hall; this information did not include anything about Hiroshima and Nagasaki. Cohen's comments (*Bombshell*, 149) show that this was the fourth Sunday in a row that she had gone to UNM looking for Hall. Hence, by deduction, we can fix the date of the UNM meeting between Cohen and Hall as Sunday, August 5 (Monday, August 6 in Hiroshima); the first attempt must have been on July 15.

Chapter Seven

1. In his confession, Harry Gold said that Fuchs picked him up near a "large church" on the edge of Santa Fe, and then they drove up into the hills overlooking the town. The spot that best fits the description and would be logical from an operational standpoint is the Scottish Rite Temple, located at Paseo de Peralta and Bishop's Lodge Road. In relation to the Santa Fe Plaza, the Scottish Rite Temple is at the twelve o'clock position, compared to the four o'clock position of their June 2 meeting spot at the Paseo de Peralta Bridge. Since Gold was on foot, both spots were equidistant from the plaza and easy walks.
2. Allen Weinstein and Alexander Vassiliev, *The Haunted Wood*, 214.
3. Ibid., 215.

Chapter Eight

1. John Earl Haynes and Harvey Klehr, VENONA: *Decoding Soviet Espionage in America*, (New Haven, CT: Yale University Press, 1999).
2. Robert Chadwell Williams, *Klaus Fuchs: Atom Spy*.
3. John Earl Haynes and Harvey Klehr, VENONA, 55.
4. Aleksandr Feklisov, *The Man Behind the Rosenbergs*, 233-94.
5. Joseph Albright and Marcia Kunstel, *Bombshell*, 212-33.
6. Allen Weinstein and Alexander Vassiliev, *The Haunted Wood*, 291.

7. John Earl Haynes and Harvey Klehr, *venona*, 329–30.
8. Pavel Sudoplatov and Anatoli Sudoplatov, *Special Tasks*, 188–96.
9. Joseph Albright and Marcia Kunstel, *Bombshell*, 271.
10. Robert Louis Benson and Michael Warner, eds., *venona*, 387–89.
11. Allen Weinstein and Alexander Vassiliev, *The Haunted Wood*, 190–92.

Chapter Nine

1. Milt Bearden and James Risen, *The Main Enemy: The Inside Story of the CIA's Final Showdown with the KGB* (New York: Random House, 2003), 3–31.
2. John Lewis Gaddis, *The Cold War: A New History* (New York: Penguin Books, 2007), 226–27.
3. Milt Bearden and James Risen, *The Main Enemy*, 29.
4. David Wise, *The Spy Who Got Away: The Inside Story of Edward Lee Howard* (New York: Random House, 1988).

Chapter Ten

1. Kirsten Lundberg, *The Anatomy of an Investigation: The Difficult Case(s) of Wen Ho Lee*, with sponsors Philip Heymann and Jessica Stern. (Harvard Kennedy School of Government Study Case Program, Reference #1641.)
2 Dan Stober and Ian Hoffman, *A Convenient Spy: Wen Ho Lee and the Politics of Nuclear Espionage* (New York: Simon and Schuster, 2001), 62–66.
3. Notra Trulock, *Code Name Kindred Spirit: Inside the Chinese Nuclear Espionage Scandal* (New York: Encounter Books, 2003), 126–27.
4. Kirsten Lundberg, *The Anatomy of an Investigation*, 15–16.
5. Ibid., 32–35.
6. Ibid., 37–38.
7. Wen Ho Lee, *My Country Versus Me: The First Hand Account of the Los Alamos Scientist Who Was Falsely Accused of Being a Spy*, with Helen Zia. (New York: Hyperion Press, 2001), 75–83.
8. Kirsten Lundberg, *The Anatomy of an Investigation*, 40–47.
9. Ibid., 67–70.
10. Sarah Garland, "Trapped in a Spy Hunt," *Newsweek Magazine*, February 7, 2009.

Index